JEWISH LONDON

JEWISH LONDON

Linda Zeff

PIATKUS

Acknowledgements

This book was compiled with a great deal of help from my family
and friends, to whom I am very grateful. I would particularly
like to thank Barbara Lantin, Milly Lewy and Jan Shure for
their advice; Solomon Jacobson for his concern; Colin Allen and
his family for their support; Annette, Robin and Chloe Bloom
for letting me empty their bookshelves; and my parents, Helen
and Mick Zeff, for their invaluable help with the research.

The author and publishers have made every effort to ensure that
all the information in this book is accurate at the time of going to
press. However, no guide-book can ever be completely up to
date. Any correspondence in connection with *Jewish London*
should be addressed to Linda Zeff, c/o Piatkus Books,
5 Windmill Street, London W1P 1HS.

© 1986 Linda Zeff
First published in 1986 by
Judy Piatkus (Publishers) Limited

Designed by Paul Saunders
Cartoons by Nero (Harry Blacker)

British Library Cataloguing in Publication Data

Zeff, Linda
  Jewish London.
  1. London (England)—Description—1981–
  —Guide-books
  I. Title
  914.21′04858   DA679

ISBN 0–86188–528–7
ISBN 0–86188–539–2 Pbk

Phototypeset in 10/12pt VIP Plantin by
D. P. Media Limited, Hitchin, Herts
Printed and made in Great Britain by
The Bath Press, Bath, Avon

Contents

Introduction

The idea for this book came from a group of American Jewish visitors to London. They'd heard of the Jewish Museum at Woburn House, they said, but was there anything else to see? They'd heard, too, of the famous Bloom's restaurant in Whitechapel, but was there anywhere else they could get a kosher meal?

The answer to both questions is, of course, 'yes'. London, the main centre of Jewish life in Britain since the Norman Conquest of 1066 and home to around 250,000 Jews today, is full of Jewish sights and sounds – not to mention salt beef and latkes!

So armed with pen and paper, and wearing my most comfortable walking shoes and best telephone voice, I began my own sightseeing and fact-finding tour of Jewish London, with the intention of compiling what I hoped would be both a useful guide-book for tourists and an informative directory for Jewish Londoners.

I began in the main Jewish areas of North-West London and Ilford but soon discovered that kosher food and wine, Jewish books and religious items are available throughout the capital, from tiny specialist shops to high-street supermarket chains, from market stalls to department stores.

I learned that there were over 160 synagogues in and around London, ranging from Orthodox to Progressive, from Britain's oldest synagogue – Bevis Marks, which dates back to 1701 – to stunningly modern buildings.

I found an astonishing number of works by Jewish artists and on Jewish themes in many of London's major art galleries, while exhibits in London's museums range from recreated scenes of Jewish life in the East End at the turn of the century to a waxwork model of David Ben-Gurion, Israel's first Prime Minister.

I came across Jewish theatre in all its forms – traditional, modern, Yiddish – as well as orchestras and dance troupes, newspapers and magazines, clubs and societies for every age group and interest.

My research had a snowball effect. Every time I thought I had completed a section I'd come across an entry that would lead me off in yet another direction. It became harder and harder to decide just how much information should be included in the book. In the end it came down to space.

I hope, however, that on the following pages you'll find *nearly* all you need to know about Jewish London (the major communal organizations listed will be able to give you details of any subjects not covered in the book); that the information I've given will at least whet your appetite; and that on your journey through Jewish London you'll make as many new friends as I have.

Linda Zeff
February 1986

London Postal Districts
(For map please see pages 4 and 5)

NORTH LONDON

N1 Islington, St Pancras
N2 East Finchley, Hampstead
  Garden Suburb
N3 Finchley
N4 Finsbury Park
N5 Highbury
N6 Highgate
N7 Holloway
N8 Hornsey & Wood Green
N9 Lower Edmonton
N10 Muswell Hill
N11 New Southgate
N12 North Finchley,
  Woodside Park
N13 Palmers Green
N14 Southgate, Cockfosters
N15 South Tottenham
N16 Stoke Newington,
  Stamford Hill
N17 Tottenham
N18 Upper Edmonton
N19 Upper Holloway
N20 Whetstone
N21 Winchmore Hill
N22 Wood Green
NW1 Camden Town,
  Regents Park
NW2 Cricklewood,
  Dollis Hill
NW3 Hampstead, Swiss
  Cottage, Belsize Park
NW4 Hendon
NW5 Kentish Town
NW6 Kilburn,
  West Hampstead
NW7 Mill Hill
NW8 St John's Wood
NW9 The Hyde, Maida Vale,
  Kingsbury
NW10 Willesden and
  Brondesbury Park

NW11 Golders Green,
  Temple Fortune, Brent

WEST LONDON

W1 Mayfair, Oxford Street,
  Soho
W2 Paddington, Bayswater
W3 Acton
W4 Chiswick
W5 Ealing
W6 Hammersmith
W7 Hanwell
W8 Kensington
W9 Maida Vale
W10 North Kensington
W11 Notting Hill
W12 Shepherd's Bush
W13 West Ealing
W14 West Kensington
WC1 Bloomsbury
WC2 Covent Garden

SOUTH LONDON

SW1 Westminster, Victoria
SW2 Brixton
SW3 Chelsea
SW4 Clapham
SW5 Earl's Court
SW6 Fulham
SW7 South Kensington
SW8 South Lambeth
SW9 Stockwell
SW10 West Brompton
SW11 Battersea
SW12 Balham
SW13 Barnes
SW14 Mortlake
SW15 Putney, Roehampton
SW16 Streatham
SW17 Tooting
SW18 Wandsworth

SW19 Wimbledon
SW20 West Wimbledon
SE1 London Bridge,
  Bermondsey
SE2 Abbey Wood
SE3 Blackheath
SE4 Brockley
SE5 Camberwell
SE6 Catford, Bromley
SE7 Charlton
SE8 Deptford
SE9 Eltham

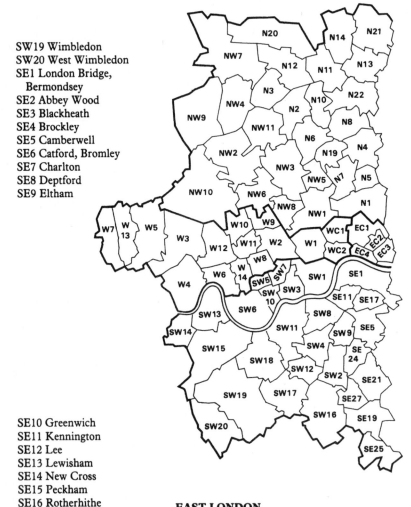

SE10 Greenwich
SE11 Kennington
SE12 Lee
SE13 Lewisham
SE14 New Cross
SE15 Peckham
SE16 Rotherhithe
SE17 Walworth
SE18 Woolwich
SE19 Norwood
SE20 Penge
SE21 Dulwich
SE22 East Dulwich
SE23 Forest Hill
SE24 Herne Hill
SE25 South Norwood
SE26 Sydenham
SE27 West Norwood
SE28 Thamesmead

EAST LONDON

E1 Aldgate, Whitechapel
E2 Bethnal Green
E3 Bow
E4 Chingford
E5 Clapton
E6 East Ham
E7 Forest Gate, West Ham,
  Upton Park
E8 Hackney
E9 Homerton
E10 Leyton

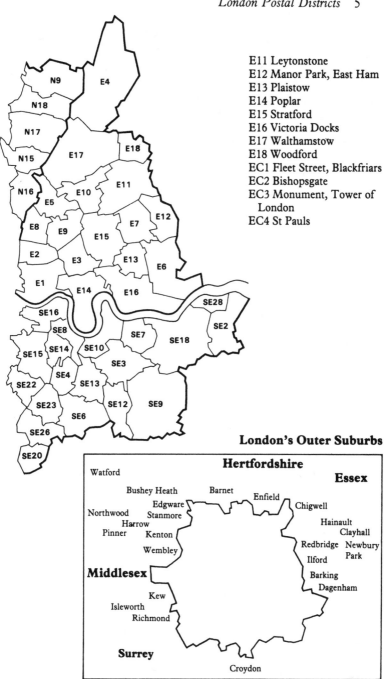

E11 Leytonstone
E12 Manor Park, East Ham
E13 Plaistow
E14 Poplar
E15 Stratford
E16 Victoria Docks
E17 Walthamstow
E18 Woodford
EC1 Fleet Street, Blackfriars
EC2 Bishopsgate
EC3 Monument, Tower of
   London
EC4 St Pauls

London's Outer Suburbs

Hertfordshire

Watford

Bushey Heath

Essex

Barnet

Enfield

Chigwell

Northwood
Edgware
Stanmore

Harrow

Pinner
Kenton

Hainault

Clayhall

Redbridge   Newbury
Park

Wembley

Ilford

Middlesex

Barking

Dagenham

Kew

Isleworth

Richmond

Surrey

Croydon

A Short History of the Jews in London

There are 250,000 Jews living in London today. They can be found in every trade and profession, from the cheeky stallholder of Petticoat Lane to the eloquent speech-maker in the House of Lords.

Jewish communities and their synagogues flourish throughout London, from the Chasidic *shtiblech* of Stamford Hill to the newer, outer-London suburban communities of Pinner, Bushey and Radlett.

Jewish newspapers and books on Jewish history and culture appear on the shelves of most high-street newsagents and bookshops; Jewish-style food has acquired quite a following (particularly bagels, salt beef and latkes!) and is obtainable from most supermarkets and delicatessens. And the contribution Jews have made to industry, the arts, science and politics is readily recognized.

But it wasn't always like this. . . .

THE EXPULSION

The history of the Jews in England begins in the 11th century, when many Jews from Rouen in Northern France came and settled in England, in the wake of William the Conqueror.

The first reference to London Jews appears in an account of the lands of the Dean and Chapter of St Paul's Cathedral of 1115, where one property is described as being 'in the Jews' street, towards St Olave's' – probably the street near the Bank of England now called Old Jewry.

Forbidden by English law to engage in most of the usual trades and professions of the time, many Jews became money-lenders (a role actually encouraged by the Church because Christians were not allowed to practise usury) and medical practitioners. They were also heavily taxed, as a clause in the so-called 'Laws of Edward the Confessor' decreed that Jews and their belongings were the sole property of the King of England.

As if this were not enough, hefty fines were also imposed on them. In 1130, for example, London Jews were fined the vast sum of £2,000 for allegedly killing a sick man who had gone to a Jewish doctor for treatment. As the Jews became more and more wealthy, they became less and less popular.

Myths about their religious practices led, in 1144, to the first blood accusation of the Jews: the case of the pretended martyr, William of Norwich. A young skinner's apprentice, he was found dead in a wood and Jews were accused of crucifying him as a ritual murder during the Passover festival. Although a number of other ritual murder accusations followed, London Jews were able to enjoy a period of relative peace, particularly when Henry II came to the throne in 1154. Henry II, the first of the Plantagenets, was said to favour and protect the Jews, whose fortunes were becoming increasingly important to the Exchequer. But that peace was to be shattered when Henry died and Richard I, known as Richard the Lionheart, came to the throne. His coronation day in 1189 marked the end of an era for the Jews of Britain.

Richard issued a proclamation that no woman or Jew should be admitted to his coronation at Westminster. But, hoping to win favour, a group of representatives of England's Jewish communities arrived at the gates bearing rich gifts. They were denied entry by a doorkeeper and a rumour quickly spread that the king had ordered all Jews to be exterminated. Several of the group were beaten or trampled to death by rioting crowds. As Richard and his party continued their celebrations, a lighted torch was used to set fire to the roof of a house in the Jewish quarter. Within a short time the whole of the Jewry was ablaze.

Thirty Jews died – some burned to death, others were stoned as they ventured into the streets. Those who escaped found refuge in the Tower of London, and later settled in the area, in a street known today as Jewry Street.

Richard then issued a charter to the Chief Rabbi giving Jews permission 'to reside in our land freely and honourably' but despite this persecution of the Jews continued until finally, on 18 July 1290, all Jews were ordered out of England by Edward I.

THE RESETTLEMENT

In 1656 Oliver Cromwell, Lord Protector, invited a well-known Amsterdam rabbi, Menasseh ben Israel, to come to England and negotiate the readmission of Jews. Many Jews were already living in London under the guise of Protestant refugees, and during the previous year Menasseh ben Israel and six London Jews had sent a petition to Cromwell, asking for permission to conduct religious services in their homes (this document can be found in the Public Records Office, see page 148).

Cromwell was in favour of resettlement. Many of the Marranos – Sephardi Jews who had been expelled from Portugal and Spain in 1492 and had settled in Holland – were cultured and wealthy, with useful overseas trading connections. Testimony from leading lawyers revealed that, contrary to general belief, there was no law forbidding Jews to return to England, since the Expulsion of 1290 had been an act of royal prerogative.

In the event, there was no formal recall of the Jews, but the small Marrano community of around 20 families felt sufficiently secure to establish a synagogue and, a couple of months later, to rent a cemetery plot. A synagogue could have been temporary, but a cemetery meant they were here to stay.

By 1688 there were more than 100 Marrano families in England, and in 1701, when their synagogue in Creechurch Lane became too small (a plaque on a wall still records the site, see page 84), they built a synagogue in Bevis Marks (see page 157). This, the first purpose-built synagogue in Britain, is still in use today.

Ashkenazi Jews from Central and East Europe arrived in London within a few years of the resettlement. In 1690 they established their own synagogue in Duke's Place (a plaque records this site, see page 157).

They were generally poor artisans or small traders who settled in the eastern part of the City and the adjacent areas of Houndsditch and Goodman's Fields, because it was only in these parts that they were allowed to trade. Jews, like Catholics and nonconformists, could not become freemen of the City of London, which meant that they could not engage in retail trade within its boundaries.

These were also the centres of the old clothes' trade, in which many Jews became involved. The Jewish 'old clothes man' used to roam the streets shouting 'Clothes, clothes, old clothes'. In the evenings these would be taken to a market in the Minories called Rag Fair.

When George I came to the throne he encouraged German Jews to settle in England and, by the middle of the 18th century, Ashkenazim outnumbered the Sephardim.

The Ashkenazi community established a number of communal institutions during this period, and the jurisdiction of the Chief Rabbi and membership of the United Synagogue was limited to German Jews.

THE BEGINNINGS OF EMANCIPATION

The restrictions on university education meant that Jews could not prepare to enter the professions, and the wording of the Christian oath required by anyone assuming public office excluded them from civic and political life.

But in 1831 the City of London restrictions were abolished, allowing Jewish financiers and merchants to expand. Since 1697, the Corporation of London had limited the number of Jewish brokers on the Royal Exchange to 12 out of a total of 124. They used to meet in the South-East corner, under the colonnade, in a section known for many years as 'Jews' Wall'.

In this period, too, the government recognized University College, which meant that those who could afford it could now obtain a degree and consequently enter the professions. And in 1833 a Jew was called to the Bar for the first time (see page 12).

By 1845 Jews could take up all municipal offices except enter Parliament. This was demonstrated by Lionel de Rothschild who was unable to take his seat in the Commons because he refused to take the obligatory oath, 'on the true faith of a Christian'.

In 1858, however, it was agreed that each chamber of Parliament could determine its own form of oath and, 11 years after he was first elected, Lionel de Rothschild took his seat in the Commons, becoming the first Jewish MP. Interestingly, Lionel de Rothschild did not speak once during the 15 years he represented the City of London in the Commons; he had only contrived to be elected to further the cause of Jewish emancipation.

A uniform oath was introduced two years later which meant that Jews could be raised to the peerage, and in 1885 Queen Victoria created the first Jewish peer – Lionel's eldest son, Nathaniel de Rothschild.

THE NEWCOMERS

Between 1880 and 1914 the Jewish population in Britain increased from 65,000 to 300,000 as a result of the arrival of Jews from the government-sponsored pogroms of Russia. Many had been on their way to America, the *goldeneh medina*. Instead of continuing their journey, they settled near the East London docks at which they had arrived. Over those 35 years there was an influx of around 100,000 Russian Jews into East London, mainly centred on Whitechapel.

By now the existing London community, who had in many ways become more English than the English, had moved out of the old Jewish quarters and into the suburbs. Until the early 19th century they had generally remained within half a square mile on the eastern borders of the city, but now the wealthy had begun to move into the fashionable West End. Nathan Mayer Rothschild and Moses Montefiore moved from St Swithins Lane to Piccadilly and Park Lane respectively, while other prominent Jewish families settled in Mayfair and the West Central district. The Goldsmids had moved into Marble Arch, the Mocattas into Bloomsbury, the Montefiores into Bloomsbury and Mayfair.

Middle-class groups, originally in Goodman's Fields or the Minories and later in Great St Helens and Finsbury Square, were now living in South London. From about 1860 they started to move into North London, into Canonbury and Dalston. By 1880 there were settlements as far afield as St John's Wood and Hampstead.

The newcomers, meanwhile, were housed in overcrowded ghettos and – unlike the rest of Anglo-Jewry – were Orthodox and traditional. Their arrival seemed to threaten emancipation, and the old community tried hard to dissuade them from coming. However, after the Kishinev pogrom of 1903, followed as it was by the worst era of mob violence against the Jews, the old community had no option but to welcome their kinsmen – and, if necessary, educate them in English ways.

The new arrivals had to develop new industries to create employment for themselves, or take low-paid semi-skilled jobs. Three of these new industries – tailoring, cabinet making and shoe making – proved particularly beneficial to the industrial life of Britain, as was noted by The Royal Commission on Immigration, 1902–1905.

The 1901 census registered over 90,000 'Russians and Poles' in East London; by 1911 this had grown to 106,000, not including the 20,000 Jews who arrived from Germany, Holland, Austria and Romania. The Aliens Bill of 1906 aimed to restrict entry, and until 1914 the influx of immigrants was reduced to 4,000 a year.

The East End began to burst at the seams, and an early settlement around Duke's Place expanded towards Thamesside and the City. The main thoroughfares and the streets branching off them were filled with Jewish homes and businesses, and at the peak of the immigration this area contained around 90 per cent of London's Jewish population.

The only way to escape the ghetto, many realized, was to build up a successful business. Between 1918 and 1939 hundreds of Jews moved east to Ilford, north to Clapton and Stamford Hill, and the more affluent to the north-western suburbs of Golders Green, Hendon and Edgware.

This pattern was to set the trend for post-war Jewish communities too. Much of the East End was devastated by bombing and it was to these new areas that most Jewish Londoners returned. These are the parts of London referred to in this book as 'Jewish areas', where you'll find most of the specialist shops, synagogues and activities.

A London Miscellany

Jews have played an important part in the history of London, and London Jews have played an important part in the history of the world. Just consider this selection of famous and infamous characters.

JEWISH 'FIRSTS'

Sir Ernest Cassell (1852–1921)
Financier and philanthropist, and close friend of Edward VII, he created the first London Underground Railway in 1900.

Benjamin Disraeli, Earl of Beaconsfield (1804–81)
The first Jewish-born MP to become Prime Minister (1868). His father had him baptized at the age of 13 after quarrelling with Bevis Marks Synagogue and resigning from the congregation. An accomplished novelist, Disraeli combined a literary career with his political career, and was created Earl of Beaconsfield in 1878.

Sir Francis Goldsmid (1808–78)
The first Jew to be called to the Bar, becoming the first Jewish barrister (1833). He also became the first Jewish QC (Queen's Counsel), in 1858.

Sir George Jessel (1824–83)
The first Jew to be a law officer of the Crown, as Solicitor-General (1871) and a judge, as Master of the Rolls (1873).

Joseph Moses Levy (1811–88)
A printer who established the first London penny paper – the *Daily Telegraph* – in 1855. He was succeeded by his son, Edward Levy-Lawson (Lord Burnham; 1833–1916), who developed it into one of Britain's leading newspapers.

Lily Montagu (1873–1963)
Founder of West Central Liberal Synagogue, she became the first Jewish woman minister in Great Britain when she was awarded the title of Lay Minister (1943). She was also one of the first women in England to be a Justice of the Peace.

Baron Lionel de Rothschild (1808–79)

He became the first Jewish member of the House of Commons (1858). His son, Nathaniel, 1st Lord Rothschild (1840–1915), became the first Jewish member of the House of Lords (1885).

Sir David Salomons (1797–1873)

The first Jewish sheriff (1835), alderman (1844), and Lord Mayor of London (1855–1856).

Sir Herbert Samuel (1870–1963)

The first professing Jew to become a member of the British cabinet (from 1909). He held office in the Liberal government from 1905–1916, and in the national government from 1931–1932. His memorandum to the Cabinet in 1914 concerning a British trust for the Jewish Home influenced the Balfour Declaration.

Sir John Simon (1818–97)

The first Jewish lawyer on the Common Law side, and the first to sit on the bench as an acting County Court Judge in 1858. He was made Serjeant-at-Law in 1868.

Baron Henry de Worms, Lord Pirbright (1840–1903)

The first Jew to hold Government office and the first Jew to stand as a Conservative candidate (1880).

FAMOUS PEOPLE
IN POLITICS AND PUBLIC LIFE

Helen Bentwich (1892–1972)

Chairman of the London County Council, 1956–57.

Sir Samuel Gluckstein (1880–1958)

Mayor of Westminster, 1920–21.

Leslie (Isaac) Lord Hore-Belisha (1893–1957)

British statesman, MP from 1923 and Minister of Transport 1934–37, and Minister of War 1937–40. He introduced the Belisha Beacon, the flashing beacon which stands at zebra crossings.

Rufus Isaacs, 1st Marquess of Reading (1860–1935)

Son of a London fruit merchant, became Viceroy of India, 1921–26.

Samuel Montagu, Lord Swaythling (1832–1911)

Founder of Samuel Montagu and Co, one of the most important private banks in London, he became a Liberal MP and founded the Federation of Synagogues in London in 1887.

FAMOUS PEOPLE IN RELIGIOUS LIFE

Antonio Carvajal (circa 1590–1659)

The first leader of the modern English Jewish community when it emerged into the open after the Resettlement.

Aaron Hart (1670–1756)

The first Chief Rabbi of the Ashkenazi community, 1709–56.

Benjamin Levy (died 1705)

The founder of the Ashkenazi community of London.

Jacob Sasportas (1610–98)

The first Haham (officiating rabbi of the Sephardi community) in London, 1664, but left the following year at the outbreak of the Great Plague.

FAMOUS PEOPLE
IN MUSIC, DANCE, AND DRAMA

Sir Michael Balcon (1896–1977)

British film director and producer who directed at Ealing Studios, makers of the famous Ealing films such as *Passport to Pimlico* and *The Blue Lamp*.

Lilian Baylis (1874–1937)

Took over the management of the Old Vic Theatre in 1912, promoting Shakespeare, opera and ballet on the London stage. She also managed the Sadlers Wells Theatre when it reopened in 1931.

Sir Frederick Cowen (1852–1935)

Conductor of the London Philharmonic Society.

Bud Flanagan (1896–1968)

One of Britain's most famous music-hall stars, who formed a partnership with Chesney Allen and was a member of the Crazy Gang. Born in East London, he wrote a number of songs including 'Underneath the Arches' and 'Umbrella Man'.

Dame Myra Hess (1890–1965)

A pianist who organized lunchtime concerts in London's National Gallery during the Second World War.

Sir Alexander Korda (1893–1956)

Hungarian-born film producer and director who formed London Films in 1932. His 112 films include *The Third Man* and *Anna Karenina*.

Pierre Monteux (1875–1964)

Conductor of the London Symphony Orchestra 1961–64.

Dame Marie Rambert (1888–1982)

Pioneer of modern British ballet, she opened a ballet school in London in 1920. Her company became, in 1935, the Ballet Rambert.

Sir Carol Reed (1906–76)

London-born film director whose films include *The Third Man* and *The Stars Look Down*.

Sir Landon Ronald (1873–1938)

British conductor, pianist and composer who accompanied Dame Nellie Melba. He became principal of the Guildhall School of Music 1910–38.

Joseph Rosenthal (1865–1946)

Born in East London, he became Britain's first war cameraman. He was sent to report the Boer War in 1898, and later the Boxer Uprising, the Russo-Japanese War and the First World War.

Vivian Van Damm (1889–1960)

Founded the Windmill Theatre in London in 1932.

FAMOUS PEOPLE IN SPORT

Ted 'Kid' Lewis (1893–1970)

Born Gershon Mendeloff, became British Featherweight Boxing Champion 1913, European Champion 1914, and World Welterweight Champion 1915.

Daniel Mendoza (1764–1836)

One of the most famous British boxers. Born in Aldgate, he was billed as 'Mendoza the Jew' and became Champion of All England 1792–95. He was the first boxer to be accorded Royal patronage, innovated 'scientific pugilism', which he promoted in his book, *The Art of Boxing* (published in 1789), and opened his own Academy.

FAMOUS PEOPLE IN ART, LITERATURE, POETRY AND PUBLISHING

David Bomberg (1890–1957)
Brought up in East London, he is best known for his paintings of Palestine and his daring Cubist renderings of East London scenes.

Joseph, Lord Duveen (1869–1939)
British art dealer and benefactor of the British Museum, the Tate Gallery and the National Portrait Gallery in London.

Sir Jacob Epstein (1880–1959)
Famous British sculptor who moved to London in 1905, where much of his work can still be seen. His first major commission was for the British Medical Association Building. He also sculpted busts of leading figures, including Albert Einstein and Chaim Weizmann.

Barnet Freedman (1901–58)
Internationally-acclaimed book illustrator, born in East London and a leading member of the 'second generation' of East End Artists.

Mark Gertler (1891–1939)
Artist born in Spitalfields, much of his early work is based on his Jewish family and East End background.

Edmond Kapp (1890–1978)
Painter and caricaturist, born in London, who became official artist to Unesco, 1946–47.

Baron Julius von Reuter (1816–99)
Founded Reuter's Agency. He was born in Germany but moved to London in 1851.

Isaac Rosenberg (1890–1918)

Painter and poet who was born in East London and became one of the most famous artists of the First World War. He was killed in action.

Vicky (1913–66)

German-born cartoonist, Victor Weisz, who moved to London in the 1930s. His works appeared in many leading newspapers and magazines, including the *Daily Express*, the *Evening Standard* and *The New Statesman*.

Israel Zangwill (1864–1926)

London-born writer best known for his sympathetic and humorous works depicting East End life. Originally a teacher at the Jews' Free School, he wrote books, essays on Jewish themes, made verse translations of Jewish liturgical poetry and became an enthusiastic Zionist.

(See also Historic Cemeteries, pages 164–71).

JEWISH LORD MAYORS OF LONDON

1855–56   Sir David Salomons

1865–66   Sir Benjamin Samuel Phillips

1889–90   Sir Henry Aaron Isaacs

1896–97   Sir George Faudel Phillips

1902–03   Sir Marcus Samuel, 1st Viscount Bearsted

1942–43   Sir Samuel George Joseph

1960–61   Sir Bernard Waley Cohen

CHILDHOOD MEMORIES OF THE EAST END (1920–39)

Members of a North London family recall what life was like for them as children in Mile End, E1, between the wars.

'We didn't have bathrooms in those days – we used to go to the local public baths with our soap and towels. Water was pumped in from outside the cubicles – we used to shout out "More hot water for number four" . . .'

'On Fridays my mother used to prepare the *cholent* – a dish of meat and vegetables in a pot – and take it to the baker's. For a few pence he'd cook it in his ovens and we would collect it at lunchtime on Shabbat . . .'

'In the evenings people used to meet each other walking along Whitechapel. Then they'd go to John Isaacs in Mile End Road for fish and chips and pickled cucumbers. Outside would be a man or woman selling bagels from a sack. Others would simply bring their chairs outside their doors and sit and chat . . .'

'The unemployed used to play dominoes inside the Union building in Great Garden Street. Sometimes my father would come home with his winnings – a bar of chocolate . . .'

'Tailoring workers would congregate outside the Gas Company on the corner of Great Garden Street [now called Greatorex Street] and Whitechapel to chat. If they were lucky someone would come along and offer them work . . .'

'At Pesach we used to play "Nuts" in the street – a game played with real nuts and shoeboxes . . .'

EAST END EXCITEMENT

The East End had its fair share of Jewish gangsters, including the 'Bessarabian Tigers' who preyed on fellow Jews at the turn of this century. The Bessarabian Tigers ran a protection racket and members of the gang were said to have been responsible for robbing and beating up a Russian police officer on holiday in London in 1902.

Then there was the Reubens Case, where ponces Marks and Moses Reubens were found guilty of stabbing a ship's engineer and executed on 24 May 1909.

One of the most memorable East End events was the Battle of

Cable Street. In September 1936 East End Jews and other local inhabitants banded together to fight a band of Fascists led by Oswald Mosley who had announced a plan to lead a great march through the East End on 4 October. Three thousand blackshirts mobilized in Royal Mint Street to march in four columns via Cable Street, protected by nearly 7,000 policemen. But by mid-afternoon 10,000 locals and dockers from Wapping and St George's gathered along the route, and a battle broke out when a lorry was overturned in the middle of the road. After police skirmishing, the Commissioner of Police ordered Mosley and his men to turn about.

DID YOU KNOW THAT . . . ?

. . . during the Glorious Revolution of 1688, Sir Solomon de Medina (circa 1650–1730), an English Jewish financier knighted by William III, kept the British army supplied with bread during the Duke of Marlborough's famous forced march from The Netherlands to Blenheim in Bavaria?

. . . in 1710, John Mendes da Costa was one of three London Jewish merchants who provided £30,000 for the supplies of necessities to the army in Flanders?

. . . Nathan Mayer Rothschild (1777–1836), who settled in London in 1805, helped fund the Government during the Napoleonic Wars because of his family connections abroad?

. . . the famous Joe Lyons tea-shops were created by the five sons of Samuel Gluckstein (1821–73), a German immigrant, and their brother-in-law, Barnet Salmon? The Glucksteins started as tobacco merchants in the East End, with a catering sideline for exhibitions, which developed into their first tea-shop in Piccadilly in 1894. By 1981 there were over 350 cafés throughout Britain, including the popular London Lyons Corner Houses in Coventry Street, Oxford Street, The Strand and Marble Arch.

. . . the Tesco supermarkets on high streets throughout Britain were founded by Sir John Cohen (1898–1979), who was born in

Stepney of immigrant parents? After serving in the Royal Flying Corps, Jack Cohen started work as a barrow-boy in Caledonian Road Market. He founded Tesco Stores in 1931 and by 1939 he had 113 shops, and by 1950, 20 self-service stores. He established his first hypermarket in 1976, with over 50,000 square feet of shopping area.

. . . in the 1830s, London's Belgrave Square was designed by George Basevi (1794–1845), a cousin of Benjamin Disraeli? Baṣevi was also responsible for the enlargement of the Middlesex Hospital in 1834.

. . . the Shell Oil Company was created by English industrialist Marcus Bearsted, 1st Viscount (1853–1927)? He was to become Lord Mayor of London in 1902 and was raised to the peerage in 1920.

. . . that the co-founder (with Cecil Rhodes) of De Beers Consolidated Diamond Mines, was Isaacs Barnato (1852–97), an English financier who earned his living as a conjurer before becoming an outstanding diamond magnate?

. . . Sir Misha Black OBE (1910–77) was consultant designer of both London Transport's Victoria and Jubilee Lines? Born in Russia (he was brought to East London at the age of two), he became a professor of the Royal College of Art, a trustee of the British Museum, a founder member of the Society of Industrial Artists and Designers, and a senior partner of the Design and Research Unit. He was a co-ordinator of the Festival of Britain in 1951 and the Silver Jubilee Exhibition of 1977.

Eating Out

Whatever your taste in food, you'll find no shortage of suitable eating-places in London. Whether you fancy salt beef and latkes at Britain's most famous kosher restaurant – Bloom's – or prefer to try something exotic and less familiar like a spicy Indian feast at one of London's newest Indian vegetarian restaurants, whether you want a quick plateful of fish and chips or a relaxed meal in an elegant fish restaurant, you need look no further than the selection given on the following pages.

The restaurants are divided up into areas – North, East, South and West London/West End – so you can see at a glance which ones are easy to get to. Each section is then divided into four kinds of restaurant: kosher, Jewish-style, fish and veg-etarian. If you are telephoning a restaurant from outside the London area, dial 01 before the number.

KOSHER

All these restaurants are strictly kosher and licensed by a kashrut authority (see page 25). They offer a variety of dishes, from Eastern European to Middle Eastern. The glossary on pages 25–7 will help you if you're unfamiliar with Jewish food.

According to Jewish dietary laws, milk and meat may not be consumed at the same meal or prepared together, so bear in mind that you won't be able to have butter on your bread or milk in your coffee in a kosher meat restaurant.

London is one of the few cities in the world which has *no* kosher restaurants open on Shabbat (Sabbath). Kosher restaur-ants will also be closed during Jewish festivals. Very few are open at Pesach (Passover) and it's best to check before turning up.

JEWISH-STYLE

These are restaurants serving traditional Jewish dishes but not licensed by a kashrut authority. Some have only Jewish-style dishes, others have just a few.

This section includes a growing number of Israeli restaurants featuring spicy Middle Eastern dishes such as falafel and hummous. If you are unfamiliar with this style of cooking don't be afraid to ask for explanations of the dishes.

FISH

Fish restaurants in London tend to specialize in shellfish and can be expensive. However, the majority offer a wide choice of dishes featuring 'permitted' fish. Many fish-and-chip restaurants fry their fish in the Jewish way, coated with matzo meal.

VEGETARIAN

These days most restaurants in London offer vegetarian dishes, or will do so if ordered in advance. You'll find an overwhelming selection of vegetarian restaurants throughout London – particularly in South London which has no kosher restaurants.

Vegetarian restaurants do not use any flesh, fish or fowl in their cooking, and many offer vegan dishes which exclude dairy foods and eggs too.

Vegetarian cooking is usually inexpensive, highly imaginative, filling and tasty, and ranges from salads and vegetable crumbles to more exotic dishes from India and China. Indian vegetarian restaurants usually offer a *thali* – a set meal featuring the specialities of the house – in addition to individual dishes.

All the restaurants in this section are recommended by the Vegetarian Society (53 Marloes Road, W8). There is also a Jewish Vegetarian Society at 'Bet Teva', 853–855 Finchley Road, NW11 (455 0692). It publishes a magazine, holds lectures and has its own restaurant (see page 29).

In addition to the restaurants featured, there are many which have a predominantly Jewish clientèle but do not fit into any of the above categories. If you like the idea of going to such a restaurant, you'll find plenty of them advertized in the *Jewish Chronicle* (see page 132).

It is also worth noting that many pizza restaurant chains, such as Pizzaland, Pizza Hut and Pizza Express, use no animal fats in their pizza bases.

Kashrut Authorities

To be classified in this book as kosher, restaurants must be supervised by one of the following authorities.

Kashrus Commission
Adler House, Tavistock Square, WC1   387 5722 and 387 5723

This is approved by the Chief Rabbi and Beth Din.

Kedassia (Joint Kashrus Committee)
40 Queen Elizabeth's Walk, N16   802 6226 and 802 6227

This is the committee of the Union of Orthodox Hebrew Congregations, Adath Yisroel synagogues and Golders Green Beth Hamedrash.

London Kashrus Board
9–11 Greatorex Street, E1   247 4471

This is the kashrut authority of the Federation of Synagogues.

Sephardi Kashrut Authority
2 Ashworth Road, W9   289 2573

The above organizations will also be able to give you names of any kosher hotels supervised by them.

Glossary of Jewish Food Terms

Every Jewish family has its own recipes for Jewish specialities, handed down from generation to generation. Similarly, the composition and spelling of the dishes served in Jewish restaurants may vary; the definitions given below should, however, give you a guide to the kind of food to expect.

Bagel or Beigel: A ring-shaped bread roll best eaten filled with smoked salmon and/or cream cheese, and the Jewish version of the traditional Sunday English breakfast.

Blintz: A paper-thin pancake, usually stuffed with sweetened cream cheese as a dessert.

Borsht: Beetroot soup.

Chopped liver: The Jewish version of liver pâté, made with calf or chicken livers, onions and hard-boiled egg. Some versions are smoother textured than others; the 'Bloom's' chopped liver is wonderfully creamy. Served as an hors d'oeuvre.

Egg and onion: An appetizer of chopped hard-boiled egg and raw onion, bound with chicken fat.

Gefilte fish: Chopped fish with onion, bound together with egg and matzo meal and served fried (hot or cold) or boiled (usually warm). Served as an appetizer or a main dish.

Halva: A very sweet almond dessert.

Kneidlach: Soup dumplings made with egg, fat and matzo meal. Some versions are lighter than others. Served in chicken soup.

Kreplach: Finely rolled-out dough filled with meat and cut into tiny squares (like ravioli) to be served in chicken soup.

Latkes or Lutkas: Very popular accompaniment, served in place of chips; a tasty fried mixture of grated potato, egg, flour and seasoning.

Lockshen: Noodles served in soup. Also mixed with sugar, sultanas, cinnamon, margarine and eggs to make lockshen pudding, a traditional Jewish dessert.

Matzo: Unleavened bread, eaten at Pesach (Passover), also served as an accompaniment in Jewish restaurants. Matzo meal (ground matzo) is used for coating and binding in Jewish cooking.

Salt beef: Pickled and boiled beef, usually brisket. Delicious with mustard in sandwiches (especially with rye bread), or as a main course with latkes or chips.

Tzimmas or Tsimmis: A slowly-cooked hotpot of meat, sweetened with prunes or dried pears, or carrots cooked with golden syrup or sugar.

Viennas: Small frankfurters.

Worsht (pronounced 'Voosht'): Salami.

North London/North-West London

KOSHER

Aviv
87 High Street, Edgware   952 2482
Mon–Thurs 12 noon–2.30 pm   6 pm–11 pm   Sat 7 pm–11 pm
All day Sun
Licensed   Access/Visa
Licensed by London Kashrus Board and under supervision of the Beth Din of Federation of Synagogues

Modern restaurant with relaxed atmosphere, specializing in Israeli cuisine. Hors d'oeuvres include hummous and falafel, chopped liver, avocado dip, mushroom salad, stuffed vine leaves. Traditional soups include kreplach. Main dishes include fish such as Dover sole, kebabs, mixed grill, *mezze* (a complete meal for two), moussaka and goulash. Non-meat dishes also served, such as tuna salad and cous-cous. Desserts are from sweet trolley.

Bloom's

130 Golders Green Road, NW11   455 1338
Mon–Thurs 12 noon–9.30 pm   Sun 12 noon–9.30 pm
Under supervision of the London Beth Din

Second branch of the world-famous Bloom's of Whitechapel. Opened in 1965, it offers, like its East End counterpart, enormous portions of good traditional Jewish fare such as borsht, chopped liver, gefilte fish, salt beef, latkes, gedempte meatballs – not forgetting the 'extras' like pickled cucumber and matzos. If you've still got room after that, desserts include apple strudel and lockshen pudding. Friendly, bustling atmosphere – not the place for a quiet, romantic dinner! Also take-away service.

Greenfeld's Deli and Snack Bar

14 Stamford Hill, N16   806 3978
Mon–Wed 10 am–7 pm   Thurs 9.30 am–7 pm   Fri 9 am–5 pm
Sun 10 am–7 pm
Licensed by the Kedassia

Describing itself as 'your personal chef', serves salads, hot dogs, cooked frozen foods.

The Jewish Vegetarian Society

853–855 Finchley Road, NW11   455 0692
Sun–Thurs 12 noon–2 pm   6 pm–9.45 pm
Licensed by the London Beth Din

Friendly, homely dining-room serving large selection of vegetarian dishes – egg dishes, quiche, daily 'specials', etc. At lunchtime light meals are also served, for instance jacket potatoes, snacks on toast. Desserts include mousse and bircher muesli.

Kosherina

8–9 Sentinel Square, Brent St, NW4   202 0338 and 202 9870
Mon–Thurs 12 noon–2.30 pm   5.30 pm–11 pm   Sat 1½ hours
after sunset till late   Sun 12 noon–11 pm
Under supervision of Kedassia and London Beth Din

Family-run vegetarian and fish restaurant specializing in

Oriental food and pizzas. Starters include borekas; main dishes include spicy vegetarian goulash, fish curry with vegetable pilau rice, sea bass, salmon, trout. Delicious home-made ice creams with tropical fruits make a pleasant change for dessert. Takeaway menu also available.

Pizza Pitta
119 Golders Green Road, NW11   455 8921
Sun–Thurs 11 am–11 pm   Early closing Fri
Licensed by London Kashrus Board and under supervision of the Beth Din of the Federation of Synagogues

Pine-clad pizza parlour serving a selection of vegetarian pizzas – Margherita, Romana, Pizza Pitta Egg (bread baked with eggs and spiced tomato). Also available are pitta, falafel, tahina, hummous, chips, cakes and juices.

Samis
85 Brent Street, NW4   202 2812
Sun–Thurs 12 noon–10 pm   Fri 10 am–2 pm
Sat 6.30 pm–12 midnight
Under supervision of the Beth Din and Kashrus Commission

New restaurant specializing in interesting Oriental and European dishes. Starters include hummous, falafel and tahina; main courses feature saloni (a fish dish), shish kebabs, steak, and 'the first kosher shawarma in London' (open roasted shoulder of lamb). Desserts include mousse, fruit salad and gâteaux, and there is a special menu for children.

Zaki's
634 Finchley Road, NW11   458 2012
Sun–Fri 12 noon–2.30 pm   Sun–Thurs 6 pm–11 pm
Sat evenings in winter
Licensed   All major credit cards
Licensed by London Kashrus Board and under supervision of the Beth Din of Federation of Synagogues

Taverna-style family-run restaurant specializing in Middle-Eastern cuisine. Hors d'oeuvres include fried aubergine, stuffed vine leaves, almond rice with raisins, lentil or vegetable soup. Main courses feature fish dishes, such as Dover sole and croquettes, as well as kebabs, mixed grill, lamb chops and a large range of Middle-Eastern specialities. Desserts include baklava and Zaki's rishta (vermicelli baked with honey and almonds). If you want to try a selection of dishes, opt for the *mezze*, a complete meal for two. A take-away menu offers such dishes as falafel and kebabs, and there's a quick lunch menu which includes Zakburgers and fish and chips.

JEWISH-STYLE

B & K Salt Beef Bar
11–13 Lanson House, Whitchurch Lane, Edgware   952 8204
Tues–Sun 12 noon–9 pm
Visa/Luncheon vouchers

Despite the name has a fairly large seating area and serves a wide range of Jewish dishes. Hors d'oeuvres include smoked salmon, gefilte fish; soups include favourites such as lockshen; entrées include fish (gefilte, fried haddock, etc), omelettes, salt beef, viennas, grills (eg kebabs) and poultry. Accompaniments include latkes, kishka, Continental salads. There's also a cold buffet and sandwiches. Desserts include halva, apple strudel. Take-away is available between 10.30 am and 9.30 pm, and there's a minimum charge in the restaurant at weekends.

The Beeferie
76 Willesden Green, NW2   459 6936
Mon–Thurs 12 noon–3 pm   6 pm–9 pm
Fri–Sun 12 noon–4 pm

Mixture of Israeli and Jewish traditional dishes available. For starters try a home-made soup such as bean and barley, or perhaps egg and onion or chopped herring. Main dishes include salt beef, viennas, fried or boiled gefilte fish, as well as house specialities of hummous, falafel and pitta, and Greek salad. Desserts include lockshen pudding, Turkish delight and pistachio halva. Turkish coffee, matzos and wholemeal pitta are also on the menu, as are daily 'specials'. Also take-away.

Continental
293 Finchley Road, NW3 794 7924
Mon–Wed 6 pm–2 am Thurs 6.30 pm–3 am
Fri 6.30 pm–2 am Sat, Sun 1 pm–4 pm
Licensed Access/American Express/Visa

Extensive menu featuring Israeli specialities such as falafel in pitta, chopped liver, Israeli salad for starters; egg, meat, chicken and fish dishes including Moroccan-style for a main course, all served with rice or chips and salad. Side orders include falafel and hammousin; desserts include halva and Greek cakes; and drinks include mint tea, wine and beers.

Eilat
2a Burroughs Parade, NW4 202 6403
Mon–Fri 12 noon–3 pm Sat, Sun 12 noon–12 am (last orders)
Licensed American Express

Specializes in Israeli dishes, with starters like hummous and falafel, soups like lockshen and kneidlach, main dishes like vegetable cous-cous and vegetarian *mezze* (a complete meal for two, which includes half a carafe of wine). Israeli salad, Turkish salad and sandwiches also available, plus more familiar (to many) dishes such as hamburgers, chicken and trout. Also take-away.

The Falafel House
95 Haverstock Hill, NW3 722 6187
Mon–Sat 6 pm–12 midnight
Visa
Egon Ronay recommended

Cosy, candlelit restaurant featuring selection of Middle-Eastern dishes including spicy bean soup, hummous and tahina, taramasalata, falafel, aubergine purée, cous-cous, latkes. Selection of salads, including Israeli salad. Also offer a *mezze* so you can try out a whole range of their specialities. Desserts include baklava, brandy trifle with cream, followed by Turkish coffee.

Harry Morgan

31 St John's Wood High Street, NW8   722 1869
Tues, Wed, Thurs 12 noon–3 pm   6 pm–10 pm
Fri 12 noon–3 pm   Sat 12 noon–3 pm   6 pm–10 pm
Sun 12 noon–10 pm

Restaurant and delicatessen, with large selection of traditional starters including calves' foot jelly, chopped liver, egg and onion, kneidlach and kreplach soup. Entrées include cold gefilte fish, haddock, worsht and eggs, salt beef, viennas, latkes, tzimmas. Desserts include lockshen pudding. Also offers selection of sandwiches.

Jimmy's Salt Beef Restaurant

301 Hale Lane, Edgware   958 4955
Sat–Thurs 11 am–9.30 pm
Licensed

Family restaurant specializing in Jewish-style cuisine 'just like mama used to make'. Starters such as chopped liver, calves' foot jelly, taramasalata; soups like beans and barley and borsht. Entrées include salt beef, tongue, gedempte meatballs, gefilte fish, omelettes, chicken, turkey schnitzel, fried or grilled fish and grills. Accompaniments include new green or sweet and sour cucumbers, Continental salads and latkes. Few seasonal 'specials', including salmon, stuffed marrow, cold pastrami salad. Selection of desserts such as halva and lockshen pudding. Take-away menu too.

Lindy's Restaurant

887 Finchley Road, NW11   455 1035
Mon–Fri 10.30 am–11.30 pm   Sat 10 am–12 midnight
Sun 12 noon–12 midnight
Licensed   Access/Visa

Large menu offers selection of Jewish-style dishes including salt beef and latkes, worsht and eggs, and gefilte fish. Interesting ice cream specialities.

Myer's
4 Halleswelle Parade, Finchley Road, NW11   455 0838
Sun–Fri 9 am–12 midnight   Sat 9 am–3 pm
Licensed   Access

Restaurant and deli serving everything from morning coffee and afternoon tea to take-away hot salt beef. Modern, cheerful décor and extensive menu. Hors d'oeuvres include smoked salmon, chopped herring, fried or boiled gefilte fish. Soups include kreplach, beetroot borsht and potato. Hot and cold fish, such as grilled Dover sole, cold fried haddock or plaice. Egg dishes include worsht and eggs. Salads such as tuna, quiche, roast beef; 'special' for slimmers and vegetarians which includes raw fruits and vegetables. Entrées include salt beef, tongue, lamb cutlets, chicken liver risotto, gedempte meatballs. Desserts include lockshen pudding, halva, apple strudel, sorbets.

Sunset
22 Ballards Lane, N3   346 3938
Mon–Sun 12 noon–10 pm
Licensed   Access/Visa

Large menu features selection of Jewish-style and Continental dishes such as salt beef and latkes, chopped liver, egg and onion, kebabs, gefilte fish, hummous, viennas, kreplach and kneidlach. Take-away section includes hot salt beef sandwiches.

FISH

Beau-Rivage
248 Belsize Road, NW6   625 6786 and 328 9992
Tues–Sat 12 noon–2.30 pm   5.30 pm–12.30 am
Sun 5.30 pm–12.30 am
Licensed for wine   Visa
Good Food Guide recommended

French cuisine, with such dishes as salmon in champagne sauce, fried Dover sole fillets with mange-tout, Israeli carp with honey dressing, poached halibut provençale, wild salmon with yogurt sauce. Fish purchased daily from Billingsgate fish market.

C & A Fish Bar
10 Bell Lane, NW4   202 9665
Mon–Sun 11.15 am–10 pm

Serves cod, haddock and plaice fillets, whole plaice on the bone, haddock cutlets, Dover sole, gefilte fish – fried fresh in oil, egg and matzo meal.

Crispins
2 Hampden Square, N14   368 2003
Mon–Sat 11.30 am–2.30 pm   4.30 pm–11.30 pm

Fish-and-chip restaurant and take-away. Fish fried in matzo meal on request.

Fogareiro
16–18 Hendon Lane, N3   346 0315
Mon–Fri 12 noon–3 pm   6 pm–11 pm   Sat 6 pm–11 pm
Licensed   All major credit cards

Portuguese and French cuisine, with Dover sole, haddock, plaice and salmon always on menu. Booking advisable. New Year's Eve dance.

La Carpa D'Oro
40 The Broadway, NW7   906 3493
Tues–Sat 11.30 am–3 pm   5.30 pm–11 pm
Licensed   All major credit cards

All fish is bought daily from Billingsgate and fried in ground nut oil and matzo meal. Starters include grilled sardines, smoked salmon, tuna and anchovy pâté. Main dishes include haddock, trout, Dover sole, lemon sole, halibut. Selection of salads, eg smoked trout and smoked salmon. Desserts include cassata, fresh cream cakes, fresh fruit salad.

Nautilus
27–29 Fortune Green Road, NW6   435 2532
Mon 11.30 am–2.30 pm   5 pm–11.30 pm   Tues 5 pm–11.30 pm
Wed–Sat 11.30 am–2.30 pm   5 pm–11.30 pm
Licensed

One of London's best-known fish restaurants, with a large Jewish following. Greek-owned, it offers all fish prepared in matzo meal and fried in ground nut oil. Starters include soup, cod's roe and grapefruit. Main dishes include Dover sole, rainbow trout, haddock, cod, plaice, etc, all served with chips. Small range of salads, eg cheese salad. Limited selection of desserts, including fruit cocktail, ice cream, or cheese and biscuits. Take-away section next door.

New Enterprise Fish Bar
157 Burnt Oak Broadway, Edgware
Mon–Wed 11.30 am–9 pm   Thurs–Sat 11.30 am–10 pm

Offers gefilte fish as well as fried fish in matzo meal to take away.

Olive Branch
267 Kilburn High Road, NW6   625 8734
Mon–Sat 12 noon–3 pm   Mon–Sat 6 pm–11.30 pm
Licensed   Visa
Good Food Guide recommended

Fish and vegetarian restaurant with varied and very interesting menu. Lunchtime dishes change daily and feature omelettes, jacket potatoes, salads, vegetable casseroles, nut loaf, vegetarian paella. Set price for three courses. The dinner menu offers dishes from around the world: starters include tabbouleh, soup, aubergine caviar, green herb mousse; main dishes, served with brown rice and salad, include vegetable curry, tuna crêpe mornay, spinach/seaweed crêpe, savoury crumble, grilled Dover sole; deserts include sesame halva, syllabub, natural fruit sorbet. Children's helpings at weekends.

Redfords
126 Golders Green Road, NW11   455 2789
313 Hale Lane, Edgware   958 2229
Mon–Sat 12 noon–2.30 pm   5.30 pm–10.30 pm
Sun 12 noon–3 pm   5.30 pm–10.30 pm
Licensed   Access/Eurocheque/Visa   Air-conditioned

Modern comfortable restaurants specializing in fish freshly-fried in matzo meal and pure nut oil. Large menu (for both branches) features Jewish-style starters like egg and onions, boiled gefilte fish, fresh salmon cocktail. Soups like borsht (hot or cold) and smetana 'with all the bits'. For entrées try fried haddock, plaice, cod, lemon sole, Dover sole, or gefilte – all served with an enormous portion of chips. Various types of Dover sole, salads (like chopped herring, cottage cheese with peach, etc), pasta. Desserts include cheesecake, pecan pie, real sherry trifle. Wines and beers. Special three-course lunch Monday to Friday. Children's portions all at half price. Take-away section. Uses only permitted products.

Sea-Shell
49–51 Lisson Grove, NW1   724 1063 and 723 8703
Tues–Sat 12 noon–2 pm   5.15 pm–10.30 pm
Licensed for wine
Egon Ronay/Good Food Guide recommended

Very popular fried fish and chip restaurant, as queues for take-away testify. Price of fish includes portion of chips. Cold fish for take-away fried in matzo meal.

VEGETARIAN

Bombay Gate
46 Market Place, Falloden Way, NW11   458 7305
Mon–Sun 12 noon–3 pm   6 pm–11 pm   Open bank holidays
Licensed

Indian vegetarian restaurant using no animal fats, eggs or fish in its dishes. Authentic cuisine features starters like onion bhajia (onion deep-fried in chickpea flour), samosas (crispy vegetable parcels), bhel poori (deep-fried breads and noodles served with chopped onion, puffed rice, coriander and chutney). Main courses include *thali* (a set meal featuring selection of dishes) and biryani (spiced rice cooked with vegetables). Desserts include kulfi (exotic ice cream) and shrikhand (a creamy dish flavoured with lemon and cardamom).

Diwana Bhel Poori House

114, 121 and 123 Drummond St, NW1   387 5556
Mon–Sun 12 noon–12 midnight
American Express/Diners/Visa
Egon Ronay/Good Food Guide recommended

Indian vegetarian restaurant serving traditional South Indian dishes such as bhel poori (see opposite), samosas, vegetable curries, bhajia (vegetables cooked in chilli and spices), *thali*, kulfi. Daily 'special' dish. Another branch at 50 Westbourne Grove, W2.

Earth Exchange

213 Archway Road, N6   340 6407
Fri–Tues 12 noon–3 pm   6 pm–10.30 pm
Egon Ronay recommended

Rustic-style café specializing in wholefood vegetarian cooking and vegan dishes. Salads, soups, main courses like nut roast, chilli, vegetable cous-cous, mushroom stroganoff, sugar-free desserts. Wide range of herb teas and organic wine. Cabaret on Monday evenings. Take-away.

Green Cottage II

122a Finchley Road, NW3   794 3969
Mon–Sun 12 noon–3 pm   6 pm–11.30 pm   Closed Tues
Licensed   Access/American Express/Diners

London's first Chinese vegetarian restaurant. Sophisticated, relaxed atmosphere. Authentic Zhai cuisine features a selection of unfamiliar flavours and textures: starters include Zhai shark's fin soup (made from Chinese vermicelli); huge range of main courses includes The Eight Treasures, a blend of diced vegetables in a spicy sauce. Presentation of the dishes is as attractive as the names of the dishes. Booking recommended.

Jai Krishna

161 Stroud Green Road, N4   272 1680
Mon–Tues 12.30 pm–2 pm   Wed–Fri 12.30 pm–2 pm
5.30 pm–10 pm   Sat 11.30 am–10 pm

Indian vegetarian restaurant offering large selection of traditional dishes including *thali* (set meal), range of different
curries, bhel poori (deep-fried breads and noodles served with
chopped onion, puffed rice, coriander and chutney), samosas
(deep-fried vegetable parcels), etc. Booking recommended.

Manna
4 Erskine Road, NW3   722 8028
Mon–Sun 6.30 pm–12 midnight
Licensed
Egon Ronay/Good Food Guide recommended

Wholefood vegetarian restaurant with rustic décor and day's
menu chalked on blackboard. Lacto-vegetarian wholefood,
includes spinach lasagne, Malaysienne bean casserole, leek and
potato pie, cheese and mushroom flan. Large selection of salads,
wonderful wholemeal rolls, delicious puddings such as
crumbles, ice creams. Some spirits available. Bookings not
accepted. Can ring for daily menu.

Rani
3–5 Long Lane, N3   349 4386
Tues–Fri 12 noon–2 pm   Mon–Sun 6 pm–10.30 pm
Closed Mon lunchtime
Licensed   Access/Eurocheque/Visa

Indian vegetarian restaurant serving pure vegetarian dishes
without fish or eggs. Family-run, with Gujarati and South
Indian home-style cooking. Selection of hot or cold starters
including samosas (pastry filled with spicy vegetables) and
bhajias (mixture of potato and onion, deep-fried in wheatflour).
Main courses include *thali*, consisting of lentil soup, plain rice,
two vegetable curries, chapatis, yogurt and pickle. Daily
specials include banana, spinach and tomato curry. Drinks
include falooda (a rose-flavoured milkshake) and sweet or salted
lassi, a cold yogurt drink. Booking recommended. Take-away
service.

Ravi Shankar

133–135 Drummond Street, NW1   388 6458
Mon–Sun 12 noon–11 pm
Wine licence
Egon Ronay/Good Food Guide recommended

Specializes in South Indian vegetarian dishes including their speciality of Mysore *thali* – a complete meal consisting of four small dishes of varying hotness served with rice, puffed-up crispy poori breads, plus an Indian doughnut in sweet syrup for dessert. Also good selection of wine and freshly-squeezed juices.

Woodlands

402 High Road, Wembley   902 9869
Mon–Sun 12 noon–3 pm   6 pm–11 pm
Licensed   All major credit cards

South Indian vegetarian restaurant, one of a chain, serving traditional dishes such as idli, dosa, medu vada, pav bhaji, lemon rice. Helpful waiters will suggest combinations of dishes for those unfamiliar with this style of cooking, which features interesting crispy pancakes with savoury fillings. Booking is advisable.

East London/East End/Essex

KOSHER

Bloom's

90 Whitechapel High St, E1   247 6001
Sun–Thurs 11 am–10 pm   Fri 11 am–3 pm
Under supervision of the London Beth Din
Wine licence   Access
Good Food Guide recommended

Britain's most famous kosher restaurant, opened in Whitechapel by Morris Bloom in 1920. Portions of their popular

Jewish fare – which includes borsht, chopped liver, gefilte fish, gedempte meatballs and, of course, salt beef and latkes – are enormous, and side orders include pickled cucumbers and matzos. *Heimische* desserts include apple strudel and lockshen pudding – washed down, perhaps, by the house Israeli wine. The décor is functional, the atmosphere lively, and the waiters well known for their character! Take-away service includes Bloom's famous kosher worsht, viennas, etc. Car parking facilities.

The Kosher Luncheon Club

Morris Kasler Hall, Greatorex Street, E1   247 0039
Mon–Fri 12 noon–3 pm
Under supervision of the London Kashrus Board and the Beth Din of the Federation of Synagogues

Fish and dairy restaurant offering daily specials as well as an à la carte menu. Warming soups include bean and barley, tomato and rice; to follow choose from fried, grilled or steamed fish – plaice, haddock, cod, sole, etc – with chips, latkes, boiled potatoes, side salads, coleslaw. Or perhaps opt for an egg dish. Customers, say the proprietors, tend to come in on the same day every week for 'the usual': on Wednesdays it's fish soup, on Fridays minced salmon cutlets.

The Sharon

376/8 Cranbrook Road, Gants Hill, Ilford   554 2471; 554 7097
and 518 0374
Mon–Thurs 10 am–9.30 pm   Fri 10 am–2 pm
Sun 10 am–10 pm
Licensed
Under supervision of the London Beth Din

The only kosher restaurant in Ilford, this has a large menu of Jewish and Continental dishes, with daily specials ranging from Italian and French to Greek cuisine. Jewish-style hors d'oeuvres include chicken blintz; liver, egg and onion; pickled herring. Soups include kreplach, meatball, and lockshen. Selection of omelettes, fish, meat dishes including baked prime bola, roast shoulder of lamb, baked klops. Cold buffet, poultry, grills, salads including celery and pineapple. Lots of vegetables including latkes. Desserts such as stewed cherries, Israeli figs, banana split. Selection of wines and Israeli juices. Also take-away.

JEWISH-STYLE

EJ's
237 Cranbrook Road, Ilford, Essex   554 3001
Mon–Thurs 12 noon–3 pm   6 pm–11 pm   Fri 12 noon–3 pm
Sat evening until 12 midnight   Sun 12 noon–12 midnight
Licensed

Attractive restaurant with pine tables and floral cloths, specializing in Israeli cuisine. Starters include tahina (an oily paste of ground roasted sesame seeds), salad and falafel (chickpea) balls and Israeli vegetable soup. Grills include skewered meats, baked chicken in a spicy sauce, chicken schnitzel, stuffed peppers. Selection of salads: 'EJ's Special Israeli Salad', aubergine salad, Turkish salad. Desserts include gâteaux, cheesecake, fresh fruit salad. Israeli coffee. Take-away section.

The Nosherie
12–13 Greville Street, EC1   242 1591
Mon–Fri 8 am–5 pm
Licensed
Egon Ronay/Good Food Guide recommended

Long-established restaurant in the heart of Hatton Garden, London's jewellery centre, very popular and serving an authentic style of all-round Jewish cooking. All-Jewish menu features traditional soups, salt beef, grilled chicken, fried fish. Supply kosher salami, turkey, viennas; all fish is kosher.

FISH

Gow's
81 Old Broad Street, EC2   528 0530
Mon–Fri 11.30 am–3 pm
Licensed   Access/American Express/Visa
Egon Ronay recommended

Established for 100 years, and with a City 'club' atmosphere, Gow's is part of Balls Brothers Wine Bars and Wine Merchants. Starters include smoked cod's roe and home-made salmon pâté. Entrées include grilled Dover sole, grilled plaice, trout with almonds, poached halibut, fried sole goujons, and smoked haddock and egg. Also 'this month's specialities', such as fillet of sole Dublère with tomato, wine and cream sauce.

Seafresh
20–21 Sevenways Parade, Gants Hill, Ilford, Essex   550 9942
Tues–Sat 12 noon–2.30 pm   5.30 pm–9.30 pm   (Fri to 10 pm Sat to 10.30 pm)   Sun 12 noon–2.30 pm   6 pm–9.30 pm
Licensed   All major credit cards

Serves large range of permitted fish and specializes in cooking in matzo meal. 'Specials' according to season, eg fresh salmon. Large selection of starters and home-made sweets. Set lunches on Sunday.

Seashell
424–426 Kingsland Road, E8   254 6152
Tues–Fri 12 noon–2 pm   5 pm–10 pm   Sat 11.30 am–10 pm
Egon Ronay/Good Food Guide recommended

Second branch of the popular Sea-Shell of Lisson Grove, NW1. Offers cod, haddock, plaice, Dover sole, lemon sole, halibut and salmon – grilled, poached or fried. Matzo meal is used for frying all cold orders and can be requested for hot fried fish. No charge for bringing your own wine.

VEGETARIAN

The Cherry Orchard
241–245 Globe Road, E2   980 6678
Tues, Wed, Fri, Sat 10 am–8.30 pm   Thursday 10 am–2.30 pm
Egon Ronay/Good Food Guide recommended

Simple cream and green décor and a peacock stained-glass

window give a pleasant atmosphere. Selection of vegan dishes and non-sugar sweets are available; vegetarian dishes include lasagne verde, mushroom stroganoff, tofu ball salad plate, carrot and cashew nut soup. The restaurant is a co-operative run by women, with entertainment on alternate Saturdays, and exhibitions which change monthly. Outdoor seating space in garden in summer. Booking advisable for 6 or more people.

Food For Health
15–17 Black Friars Lane, EC4   236 7001
Mon–Fri 8 am–3 pm
Egon Ronay recommended

Lunchtime self-service eating-place for City vegetarians, serving over 600 people a day! Hot dishes include enormous portions of cheese soufflé, moussaka made with TVP (substitute meat), tagliatelli, puff pastry rolls and vol-au-vents, spinach and cottage cheese savoury. Delicious salads and puddings. Booking a table is recommended. Take-away section.

Slenders
41 Cathedral Place, EC4   236 5974
Mon–Fri 8 am–6.15 pm
Egon Ronay recommended

Slenders has been in the area for 16 years. Natural pine and hessian décor and piped classical music make for a relaxing atmosphere. Dishes include vegetarian salads, quiches, vegetarian casseroles. Rice and bean dishes also on the menu.

South London/Surrey

FISH

Gastronome One
311–313 New Kings Road, SW6   731 6381
Mon–Fri 12 noon–2 pm   Mon–Sat 7 pm–11 pm
Licensed   All major credit cards
Egon Ronay recommended

Has a French inn atmosphere, with log fire, beams and formally dressed waiters. Food is French cuisine nouvelle, with interesting descriptions such as *tresses de sole au beurre rouge* (braids of sole with red butter!). Shellfish is served separately. Booking advisable.

Mr Fish
393 Upper Richmond Road, SW15   876 3083
Tues–Sun 12 noon–2.30 pm   Sun–Mon 6 pm–11.30 pm
Licensed   All major credit cards
Good Food Guide recommended

Smart fish-and-chip shop serving cod, plaice, haddock, sole, etc. fried in ground-nut oil. Booking advisable.

VEGETARIAN

Beehive Place
11a Beehive Place, SW9   274 1690
Mon–Sat 10 am–5.30 pm (main meals 12 noon–3 pm)

Relaxed restaurant in a converted stable, serving vegan dishes such as aduki-stuffed tofu in ginger and shoyu sauce, butternut pumpkin soup, plum and tofu crunch, tofu and sunflower seed croquettes. Range of organic wines. Almost all ingredients used are organically grown.

The Café Upstairs
Balham Food and Book Co-op
92 Balham High Road, SW12   673 0946
Mon, Tues, Thurs, Fri, Sat 11 am–4 pm

Offers a choice of two main dishes daily, one of which is always dairy-free, plus a variety of snacks, salads and cakes. Sugar-free fruit juices and herb teas available. All dishes are made from good-quality ingredients, organically grown wherever possible. Prices are very low – under £2 for a main meal. Will also do outside catering.

Dining Room
Winchester Walk, SE1   407 0337
Tues–Fri 12 noon–3 pm   7 pm–10 pm
Wine licence
Egon Ronay/Good Food Guide recommended

Despite its austere décor, has an imaginative vegetarian/ wholefood menu, with organic produce used whenever possible. Unusual soups, gooey puddings. Licensed for beer, wine and cider. Booking a table recommended.

Di's Larder
62 Lavender Hill, SW11   223 4618
Mon–Sat 10 am–6 pm
Egon Ronay recommended

Friendly restaurant with unpretentious décor, serving vegetarian wholefood dishes. Fresh soups, eg Potage Solferino (tomato, leek and potato) followed by main courses such as courgettes stuffed with bulgar and lentils; also quiche, pizza, selection of cooked and raw salads. All food freshly prepared on the premises using only natural products. Also a wholefood shop and bakery.

Hockneys
98 High Street, Croydon, Surrey   688 2899
Tues–Sat 12 noon–10.30 pm   Closed Sun and Mon, two weeks in August and two weeks around Christmas-time
Corkage Fee   All major credit cards
Egon Ronay/Good Food Guide recommended

Adjoining The Arts Centre in Croydon, Hockneys has been described as 'rather like eating in an art gallery'. Spacious and artistic restaurant dedicated to British painter David Hockney. Hockney prints hang on the walls. Equally attractive menu includes starters such as melon with coconut and ginger sauce, pâté, dahl soup; main dishes feature lasagne, stroganoff, vegetable curry, quiche, falafel, vegetable burger, salads. Bring your own wine. Booking a table advisable. Occasional live music at weekends.

La Vida
164 Cherry Orchard Road, Croydon, Surrey   681 3402
Wed–Fri 12 noon–2 pm   Tues–Sat 6.30 pm–10.30 pm
Licensed   Access/Barclaycard

Smart international vegetarian restaurant, with background music. Booking a table advisable.

Nature's Way
140 High Street, Penge, SE20   659 0814
Mon–Sat 10 am–4 pm
Egon Ronay recommended

Vegetarian cuisine served in peaceful pine setting. Quiches, nut roasts, gratin dishes, various salads, wholemeal cakes and desserts. Hot dishes change daily. No smoking allowed.

Richmond Harvest
5 Dome Buildings, The Quadrant, Richmond, Surrey
940 1138
Mon–Sat 11.30 am–11 pm   Sun 11.30 am–10.30 pm
Licensed
Egon Ronay recommended

Italian-style restaurant offering selection of interesting English and Continental vegetarian dishes; for instance, aubergine nut crumble, bean and mushroom stroganoff, moussaka, sweet and sour mixed vegetables, walnut roast with apple sauce, red bean chilli. All food freshly prepared on the premises. Menu changes twice daily, for lunch and dinner. Booking advisable for evening meal.

Wholemeal Café

1 Shrubbery Road, SW16   769 2423
Sun–Thurs 12 noon–10 pm   Fri, Sat 12 noon–6 pm   7 pm–10 pm
Wine licence
Egon Ronay recommended

Homely natural décor. Home-made-style dishes include sunflower seed and onion soup, lentil hotpot, red bean ratatouille, celery and apple nut roast. Puddings include banana crumble, chocolate pudding, fresh fruit yogurt. Set meal, waitress service on Friday and Saturday evenings, when booking is advisable. Licensed for wine, cider and beer. Open bank holidays.

Wilkins Natural Foods

61 Marsham Street, SW1   222 4038
Mon–Fri 8 am–5 pm
Egon Ronay recommended

International vegetarian dishes served in old stripped pine surroundings. Fresh fruit and vegetable salads, vegetable soups, macrobiotic rice, French onion soup, pasta and bean dishes, various wholefood sweets with low (or no) sugar. Expect to queue at lunchtime when the restaurant is at its busiest. Tomor (kosher) margarine is used in all pastries. No booking.

Windmill Wholefoods

486 Fulham Road, SW6   385 1570
Mon–Sat 12 noon–11 pm   Sun 7 pm–11 pm
Egon Ronay recommended

Simple, homely décor with candlelight for evenings, and a mix of classical and jazz background taped music. Specializes in interesting wholefood dishes including vegetables au gratin and brown rice, aubergine crumble, nut roast, red bean goulash. Choice of six salads which change daily, and eight desserts. All food prepared daily from fresh ingredients.

Woodlands

37 Panton Street, SW1   839 7258
Mon–Sat 12 noon–3 pm   6 pm–11 pm
Licensed   All major credit cards
Egon Ronay/Good Food Guide recommended

One of a chain of South Indian vegetarian restaurants. Serves traditional dishes such as idli, dosa, medu vada, pav bhaji, all of which will be explained in detail by the waiters. This style of cooking features a selection of crispy pancakes with savoury fillings – some hotter than others. Booking advisable.

West London/West End

KOSHER

Kosher Meat Restaurant

B'nai B'rith Hillel House, 1–2 Endsleigh Street, WC1
388 0801/2
Mon–Thurs 12 noon–2.30 pm   5.30 pm–8 pm
Fri 12 noon–1 pm
Licensed
Under supervision of the Beth Din and Kashrus Commission

Self-service restaurant serving starters such as chopped liver, gefilte fish and parev (milk-free) soups; main dishes feature chicken, fish, steak, beefburgers.

Reubens

20a Baker Street, W1
Restaurant: *Mon–Thurs and Sun 12 noon–3 pm   5 pm–10 pm*
Fri 12 noon–3 pm   935 5945

Snack bar: *Mon–Thurs 11 am–10 pm   Fri 11 am–3 pm*
Sun 11 am–10 pm   486 7079
Licensed   All major credit cards
Licensed by the London Kashrus Board under the supervision
of the Beth Din of Federation of Synagogues

Snack bar and take-away downstairs, restaurant upstairs.
Tables outside in summer. Snack bar serves sandwiches (includ-
ing, of course, salt beef), burgers, kebabs, salads and desserts.
Restaurant serves such traditional dishes as helzel (stuffed
neck), chopped herring, chopped liver, lockshen soup, plus
Israeli specialities like falafel (chickpea balls), hummous, tab-
bouleh; also fish, liver, salt beef, schnitzels, latkes. Selection of
Israeli wines.

JEWISH-STYLE

Gaby's Continental Bar
30 Charing Cross Road, WC2   836 4233
Mon–Sun 9 am–12 midnight

Large café-style restaurant serving mixture of Continental dishes. Hors d'oeuvres include chopped liver, taramasalata, hummous and falafel; soups include chicken noodle, bean and barley; specialities include salt beef, viennas and chips; selection of omelettes; latkes, pickled cucumbers, aubergine salad, etc. Sandwiches include salt beef, kosher salami, salt beef 'special' with salad and pickle, chopped liver, smoked salmon – served on white, brown or rye bread. Desserts include apple strudel, ice creams. Also extensive vegetarian menu. All dishes cooked with pure vegetable oil. Also take-away.

Grahame's Seafare
38 Poland Street, W1   437 3788 and 437 0975
Mon–Sat 12 noon–2.45 pm   Tues, Sat 5.30 pm–8.45 pm (last orders)
Licensed
Good Food Guide recommended

Jewish-style fish restaurant serving salmon, sole, haddock, plaice, gefilte fish, borsht, blintzes etc. Only kosher ingredients used. Fish comes fresh from Billingsgate fish market daily and is mainly served fried in matzo meal and accompanied by chips. Booking is advisable.

Morry's Bagels
39 Coventry Street, W1   930 0404
Mon–Sat 9.30 am–3.30 am

Bagels are filled with your favourite ingredients, to eat in – there's a tiny bar with stools – or to take away. Smoked salmon (with or without cream cheese), chopped liver, chopped herring, taramasalata, salami, hot salt beef, etc. Plain or onion varieties. Also salt beef, latkes, falafels, salmon pâté, Continental salads, freshly baked cakes, tea, coffee and cold drinks.

Phil Rabin's Salt Beef Bar & Deli
39 Great Windmill Street, W1   437 8429
Mon–Sun 11 am–12 midnight

Long-established Soho salt beef bar, with a 'twin' in Chicago. Over the past 40 years has specialized in traditional Jewish fare, with hors d'oeuvres of chopped liver, smoked salmon, and kreplach and lockshen soups. Main dishes include liver and onions, chicken, hot salt beef, gefilte fish, cold pastrami and roast beef. Also serves sandwiches, salads, latkes and matzos. Desserts include halva, lockshen pudding. Take-away section.

Picnic
108 Seymour Place, W1   723 7924 and 723 2107
Mon–Fri 9 am–11 pm   Sat 10.30 am–3.30 pm
Licence applied for

Specializes in Jewish cuisine as well as serving vegetarian dishes such as falafel and tahini. Soon to be licensed for spirits. Music and Oriental dancing every Friday at 8 pm.

Sandwich Scene
155 Wardour Street, W1

Not really a Jewish-style sandwich bar, but if you're passing you can get salt beef and pitta, or vegetarian falafel here.

The Widow Applebaum's
46 South Molton Street, W1   629 4649 and 499 6710
Mon–Sat 10 am–1 am
Licensed

New York-style deli serving hot salt beef, hot pastrami, chopped liver, lox (smoked salmon) on a bagel, etc. Background of pop music; wide video screen. Late licence until 1 am.

FISH

Bentley's
11–15 Swallow Street, W1   734 4756 and 734 6210
Mon–Sat 12 noon–3 pm   6 pm–11 pm
Licensed   Major credit cards

Upmarket fish restaurant with take-away next door for cold dishes. Hot or cold starters include melon, marinade of fresh herrings with sour cream, grilled sardines, smoked salmon pâté, gravlaks (pickled smoked salmon with dill sauce). Main courses include a dozen different ways to serve Dover sole, including poached in savoury raspberry sauce, on a bed of spinach with cheese sauce, poached in wine; a selection of imaginative salmon and trout dishes, eg salmon poached with port and basil and trout boned and filled with walnut stuffing and served with walnut butter. Desserts include ices, sorbets, fresh fruit salad.

Flounders
19–21 Tavistock Street, WC2   836 3925
Mon–Sat 12.30 pm–2.30 pm   5.30 pm–11.30 pm
Licensed   All major credit cards
Egon Ronay recommended

French-style cuisine, with cod, haddock, sole and plaice dishes always on the menu. Booking advisable.

Golden Carp
8a Mount Street, W1   499 3385 and 629 5446
Mon–Fri 12 noon–3 pm   Mon–Sat 6 pm–11.15 pm
Licensed   All major credit cards
Michelin Guide recommended

Long-established fish restaurant serving international cuisine. Fish specialities depend on fish in season. Menu changes weekly. Part of a chain of wine bars, restaurants and trattorias.

The Ivy
1–5 West Street, WC2   836 4751/2
Mon–Fri 12.15 pm–2.15 pm   Mon–Sat 6.15 pm–11 pm
Licensed   All major credit cards

Part of the famous Wheeler's group of fish restaurants, The Ivy offers a wide selection of sole and fresh salmon dishes. Booking recommended.

Payton Plaice
96 Charing Cross Road, WC2   379 3277
Mon–Sat 11.45 am–11.30 pm
American Express

Started life as a fish restaurant only, but has recently changed its menu to include pasta and salads. It has a zany nautical atmosphere and is a stone's throw from Foyles bookshop and many West End theatres. Part of a chain of restaurants owned by American-Jewish Bob Payton (his Chicago Pizza Pie Factory in Hanover Square has a mezuza on the door!). It offers lemon sole, salmon trout, fried plaice and chips, 'blackened white fish' (a New Orleans spicy cod recipe) and a grilled fish of the day. Desserts are American – pecan pie, mud pie, key lime pie. Or ice cream.

Sheekeys
28 St Martin's Court, WC2   240 2565
Mon–Sat 12.30 pm–2.45 pm   6 pm–11.15 pm
Licensed   All major credit cards
Good Food Guide recommended

Convenient for a number of West End theatres, this fashionable restaurant has starters such as grilled sardines, Ogen melon and smoked salmon; main courses include grilled Dover sole, smoked haddock. Enormous wine list. Booking advisable.

Trattoria Dei Pescatori
57 Charlotte Street, W1   580 3289
Mon–Sat 12 noon–2.30 pm (except Wed)   6 pm–10 pm
Licensed   All major credit cards

Part of a chain of Italian restaurants, this offers dishes such as Dover Sole al Funghetto (in white wine, mushroom and cream sauce), Halibut alla Mugniara (in butter with fine herbs and a dash of lemon) and Trota alla Livornese (river trout cooked in butter with a white wine sauce, tomatoes, capers and olives). Booking recommended.

VEGETARIAN

Country Life
123 Regent Street Building, 1 Heddon Street, W1   434 2922
Mon–Fri 11.30 am–2.30 pm
Good Food Guide recommended

Country-style buffet serving strictly vegetarian dishes. All cheeses and sauces are made from nuts and beans, and all cooking equipment is new and has not come into contact with animal fats. Other branches in New York, Los Angeles and Japan. Offer all-you-care-to-eat specials for a set price. Self service. Take-away available.

Cranks
Covent Garden Market, WC2   379 6508
Mon–Sat 10 am–8 pm

Part of the Cranks Health Foods chain, specializes upstairs in take-away service – savoury pies, rissoles, quiches, salads, natural yogurts, wholemeal cakes, pastries, etc. But has a tiny restaurant downstairs serving freshly-extracted fruit and vegetable juices, coffee, savoury drinks, soups, wholemeal baps, savouries, sweets and cakes.

Cranks
8 Marshall Street, W1   437 9431
Tues–Sat 10 am–11 pm   Mon 10 am–8.30 pm
Wine licence   All major credit cards
Egon Ronay recommended

Offers vegetarian wholefood dishes, with raw salads a speciality. Home-made soups, savouries, eg mushroom stroganoff and vegetable crumble. Live yogurt, cinnamon fruit, pecan pie, mincemeat and apple jalousie for dessert. Car park at rear. Booking recommended for 'Dine and Wine' evening restaurant,

Tues–Sat 6.30 pm–11 pm. Classical guitar entertainment on Friday, folk guitar on Saturday, lute on Wednesdays.

Cranks
9–11 Tottenham Street, W1   631 3912
Mon–Fri 8 am–8 pm   Sat 10 am–6 pm

Newest Cranks restaurant, just opposite Heal's in Tottenham Court Road. All the usual Cranks fare (see above) available at buffet or take-away counter. The restaurant opens early for breakfast on weekdays. Space for outdoor eating in summer.

Food For Thought
31 Neal Street, WC2   836 0239
Mon–Fri 12 noon–8 pm
Egon Ronay/Good Food Guide recommended

International vegetarian restaurant with informal décor of whitewashed walls, pine tables, flowers and paintings. Delicious salads, casseroles, breads. Very lively staff!

Govinda's
9–10 Soho Street, W1   437 3662
Mon–Sat 11.30 am–11 pm
Egon Ronay recommended

Strictly vegetarian restaurant serving no meat, fish or eggs – although dairy products are often used. Dishes such as lasagne, broccoli pie, Moroccan vegetables, sweet and sour dishes, pizza, samosa, vegburger, various delicious salads and sweets. Self-service. Run by Hare Krishna followers but patronized by all.

Greenhouse
16 Chenies Street, WC1   637 8038
Tues–Fri 10 am–10 pm   Mon 10 am–6 pm   Sat 4 pm–9 pm

Simple, rustic and informal candlelit basement where you can try a wide range of interesting and varied wholefood vegetarian dishes. Vegan dishes (ie without eggs and dairy foods) always included in menu chalked on blackboard. Typical selection: watercress and orange soup, followed by barni goreng (spicy stir-fried vegetables with wholemeal spaghetti) or falafels (served with minted yogurt dressing) or aubergine and cottage cheese pâté with sesame toast. Also pizza, quiche, salads. Desserts include wide selection of wholefood cakes, pastries, cookies and ices. Fruit juices, coffee, tea and herb teas or barleycup to drink. Menu changes daily, prices very reasonable. Can bring your own wine. No bookings taken. Attached to the Drill Hall Theatre.

Hare Krishna Curry House
1 Hanway Street, W1   636 5262
Mon–Sat 12 noon–10.30 pm
Licensed
Good Food Guide recommended

Your chance to try traditional Indian vegetarian dishes to a background of recorded Indian classical music. Dishes include samosa (pastry parcels), bhatiya, masala dosa and a vegetarian *thali* (set meal). (Despite the name, this restaurant is not run by the Hare Krishna cult.)

Raw Deal
65 York Street, W1   262 4841
Mon–Fri 10 am–10 pm   Sat 10 am–11 pm
Closed bank holidays
Egon Ronay recommended

Bistro-style vegetarian restaurant with pine tables and guitarist on Tuesday and Saturday nights. Dishes include nut roast, stuffed pancakes, pasta dishes, variety of salads which change daily, home-made cakes and pastries, fresh fruit salad. Booking not necessary. You can bring your own wine – there's no corkage charge.

Woodlands
77 Marylebone Lane, W1   486 3862
Mon–Sun 12 noon–3 pm   6 pm–11 pm
Licensed   All major credit cards
Egon Ronay/Good Food Guide recommended

Elegant South Indian vegetarian restaurant serving traditional dishes such as idli, dosa, medu vada, pav bhaji, lemon rice. Helpful waiters will suggest combinations of dishes for those unfamiliar with this style of cooking which features interesting crispy pancakes with savoury fillings. Booking advisable.

Zzzzz's
238 Grays Inn Road, WC1   833 4466
Mon–Fri 8.30 am–4 pm   Sat 10.30 am–3.30 pm
Access/Visa

Situated in a pine bed shop (hence the name) serves only wholefood meals freshly made on the premises. Soups, quiches, cakes, pies, pizzas, organic bread, fruit crumbles, salads of all kinds. Fresh orange juice. Also take-away.

Shopping

Shops stocking Jewish food and wine, books and music, greetings cards and gifts, can be found all over London. Additionally, there are many specialist Jewish shops in areas where large communities have evolved, such as Edgware, Finchley, Hendon and Ilford. Here you'll find that most local newsagents stock Jewish newspapers, magazines and greetings cards, most off-licences stock kosher wines, and most grocers have a large selection of kosher packet and canned goods.

Jewish centres are usually busy on Sunday mornings, with locals out shopping for bagels, smoked salmon and cream cheese for breakfast, or hot salt beef sandwiches for lunch. In fashion-conscious Golders Green, you can even buy a new outfit on Sunday!

We cannot include every shop in London offering kosher or Jewish items, but on the following pages you'll find a very varied selection.

If you are telephoning from outside the London area, dial 01 before the number indicated.

Bakeries and Patisseries

Most people have heard of bagels, but there are a number of other delicious Jewish-style breads and rolls that these days are eaten by Jews and non-Jews alike.

Ring-shaped bagels, seeded platzels, rye bread and cholla (which is eaten at the Friday night meal) can all be found pre-packed on the shelves of local supermarkets and delicatessens. The freshest, of course, come from the bakeries themselves. (Remember that kosher and many Jewish-style bakeries close early on Fridays and are not open on Saturdays. Most open on Sunday mornings.)

KOSHER

Alfray
12a Manor Road, N16   800 1856

Licensed by the London Beth Din and Joint Kashrus Committee.

Grodzinski's
Head Office: Overbury Road, N15   802 4161

Branches at:
867 Finchley Road, NW11   455 9370
3 Halleswelle Parade, Finchley Road, NW11   455 7242
223 Golders Green Road, NW11   458 3654
2 High Road, NW10   459 2380
45 Market Place, NW11   455 0470

Shops at:
13 Brewer Street, W1   437 3302
170 Clapton Common, E5   800 2535
408 Cranbrook Road, Ilford   554 6113
91 Dunsmure Road, N16   802 4164
5 Edgwarebury Lane, Edgware   958 1205
88 Edgware Way, Edgware   958 9391
53 Goodge Street, W1   636 0561
161 Haverstock Hill, NW3   722 7688
22 Leather Lane, EC1   405 9492
9 Northways Parade, NW3   722 4944
34 Stamford Hill, N16   802 4161
62 Vivian Avenue, NW4   202 6092
235 Whitechapel Road, E1   247 8516

Licensed by the London Beth Din and Joint Kashrus Committee. Larger branches also stock groceries.

Keene's Patisserie
234b Station Road, Edgware, Middx   958 2312 (shop)
958 5553 and 958 5554 (bakery)

Branches at:
120 Ballards Lane, N3   346 5348

101 Brent Street, NW4   202 6160
98a Golders Green Road, NW11   455 2500
192 Preston Road, Wembley   904 5952
20 Station Parade, NW2   452 5231

Under supervision of the Beth Din and Kashrus Commission.

Macabi Bagel Bakery and Delicatessen
62 Upper Clapton Road, N16   806 4891

Licensed by the Joint Kashrus Committee of the Union of Orthodox Congregations of Adath Yisroel Synagogue.

Parkway Patisserie
Gateway House, 326 Regents Park Road, N3   346 0344

Branches at:
30a North End Road, NW11   455 5026
326 Regents Park Road, N3   349 1276

Under supervision of the Beth Din and Kedassia.

Ross Bakeries
54 Downham Road, N1   249 8725 (bakery)
84 Stamford Hill, N16   806 4002 (shop)

Licensed by the Joint Kashrus Committee.

Woodberry Down Bakeries Ltd
146 High Road, N15   800 4230

Branches at:
47 Brent Street, NW4   202 9962
Downs Court Parade, Amhurst Road, E8   985 8059
12 Onslow Parade, N14   368 4528
140b Upper Clapton Road, E5   806 7405
2b Woodberry Down, N4   800 6705
93 Woodberry Grove, N4   800 0152

Licensed by the London Beth Din and Joint Kashrus Committee.

JEWISH-STYLE

Bagel Bakery Ltd
42 Redbridge Lane East, Redbridge, Ilford, Essex   550 3655

Bakery, shop and delicatessen.

Beecholme Bakeries Ltd
305 Hale Lane, Edgware, Middx   958 6681 and 958 3484

Offers freshly-baked hot bagels and platzels on Saturday nights between 8.30 pm–1.30 am, filled with Scotch salmon, cream cheese and other fillings.

Ben Jacobs Patisserie
38 Vivian Avenue, NW4   202 9868

Filled hot bagels available on Saturday nights.

Golden Beigels Ltd
87 Reighton Road, E5   806 4047

Bakery and shop.

Ridley Bagel Bakery
116 Upper Clapton Road, E5   241 1047

Bakery and shop.

Kosher Chocolates

A relatively new phenomemon in London is the 'speciality chocolate shop', offering gift-wrapped Belgian cream delights which are fast becoming the thing to take to parties. Many of these shops are in predominantly Jewish areas, and the following offer a selection of kosher parev chocolates, made under supervision of the Chief Rabbi of Brussels.

Candice
190a Station Road, Edgware, Middx   951 1599

Georgie's
79 Golders Green Road, NW11   455 4481

Kate
9 Beehive Lane, Ilford, Essex   554 7760

Kristal
7 Halleswelle Parade, Finchley Road, NW11   209 1490 and
209 1499

Nadia
111 Golders Green Road, NW11   458 3632

Grocers and Delicatessens

KOSHER

Breuer and Spitzer
11 Manor Parade, N16   800 2339
101 Dunsmure Road, N16   802 2776
Licensed by Kedassia

General supermarket.

Carmel Delicatessen
145 Clapton Common, E5   800 4033
Licensed by the London Beth Din

Also does hot salt beef and sandwiches to take away.

The Kosher Gourmet
5 Canons Corner, London Road, Stanmore   958 9446
Under supervision of the London Beth Din and Kashrus
Commission

Deli and take-away. Hot salt beef, pre-cooked meats, salads,
delicatessen, decorated meat platters, stuffed peppers, etc.

Northern Stores
772 Finchley Road, NW11   455 3590
Licensed by Kedassia

Grocers.

Reich's Takeaway
10 Princes Parade, Golders Green Road, NW11
Licensed by Kedassia

Meats, latkes, bread, etc.

Steve's Kosher Delicatessen
228–230 Station Road, Edgware   958 6715
Licensed by the London Kashrus Board and Beth Din of the
Federation of Synagogues

Delicatessen, take-away and snack bar; off-license with a wide
selection of kosher wines.

JEWISH-STYLE

The following supermarkets, grocers and delicatessens stock a
number of kosher packet or canned goods, wines or Jewish-style
delicatessen items such as gefilte fish, latkes, etc.

Alan Flax & Co
459 Finchley Road, NW3   435 3102

Grocers.

Bejam
A chain of freezer food centres. The following branches offer
frozen kosher food: East Finchley, Edgware, Gants Hill,
Ilford, Kingsbury, Southgate, South Woodford, Stanmore,
Streatham, Whetstone.

Berger and Tiversky Ltd
11 Amhurst Parade, N16   800 4691

Grocers stocking bagels, matzot, etc. Also wines, beers and
spirits.

Bernie's Delicatessen
21–23 Station Road, Edgware, Middx   952 1846

Worsht, viennas, hot salt beef and sandwiches, fried and gefilte
fish, etc.

Broer's
Highview Parade, Woodford Avenue, Ilford   550 9588

Grocers with bakery and deli section and kosher off-licence.

Cohen and Kelly
23 Brook Parade, Chigwell High Road, Chigwell, Essex
501 2864

Delicatessen offering Jewish-style and kosher food including worsht (salami), etc.

Continental Delicatessen Stores
142a Upper Clapton Road, E5   806 5073

Grocers.

Country Market
140 Golders Green Road, NW11   455 3595

Supermarket with large selection of kosher and Jewish-style food including wines.

Damazer Delicatessen
1d Walm Lane, NW2   459 2336

Frohwein's food – salami, viennas and sausages – and packeted and canned items such as noodles and soups.

M. Davis
9 Hampden Square, N14   368 6258

Grocers/delicatessen.

The Deli
394 Uxbridge Road, Hatch End, Middx   428 4929

Deliphone
167 Longwood Gardens, Clayhall, Essex   551 3530

Large delicatessen with coffee lounge (called 'The Beckery') at the back, serving salads, snacks, tea and coffee and take-away section. Will serve any foods sold on the deli counter.

The Egg Stores Ltd
4 Stamford Hill, N16   806 2266

Sells groceries and household goods. Jewish-style foods offered include worsht (salami), schmaltz herrings (herrings soaked in brine).

Flax's Delicatessen
15 Russell Parade, NW11   455 5633

Food Glorious Food
4 Church Road, Stanmore, Middx   954 7233

Delicatessen stocking bagels and platzels, Bloom's kosher foods, smoked salmon, hot latkes, sweet and sour herrings, spicy Sephardi-style savoury pies, fish balls, salads, cheeses, French patisserie.

Frosts Supermarket
24–26 Golders Green Road, NW11   458 8258

Herrings, kosher sausages and biscuits, latkes, fish balls, fish goujons and a range of kosher frozen food.

Green Brothers (Delicatessen) Ltd
56 Market Place, Hampstead Garden Suburb, NW11
458 1878

Supermarket and delicatessen.

John's Foodland's
46 Stamford Hill, N16   806 2757

Sells smoked salmon, matzo meal, vermicelli, dills for cooking,
etc.

Kaplan's
48 Vivian Avenue, NW4   202 8507

Delicatessen/grocer.

Kays Delicatessen
2 Princes Parade, Golders Green Road, NW11   458 3756

Korona Delicatessen
58 Streatham High Road, SW16   769 6647

Sells Continental and Jewish-style food.

Lenny Miller
Clayburn Broadway, Clayhall, Essex   550 6350

Delicatessen with large selection of kosher cheeses, gefilte fish,
packets and cans, etc. Also has a frozen food centre a few doors
away with enormous kosher selection.

Malde Supermarket
9 Glengall Road, Edgware, Middx   958 4744

Osem and Telma, Bloom's and Empire kosher products – cans,
packets, lockshen, sausages, etc.

Marks Delicatessen
37 Market Place, NW11   455 9013

M. Marks & Sons (Fisheries) Ltd
57 Wentworth Street, E1   247 1400 and 247 4294

Deli/grocers specializing in every kind of herring – in soured cream, wine, soused, pickled, schmaltz, etc – plus home-cured smoked salmon.

Martin's Delicatessen
33 Vivian Avenue, NW4   202 7336

Mautner
147 Deans Lane, Edgware, Middx   959 3762

Small supermarket stocks a selection of kosher packets, cans and pre-packed meats, plus kosher wines.

Moses Supermarket
182 Stamford Hill, N16   800 1883

Moshe Kosher Food Specialist
1099 Finchley Road, Temple Fortune, NW11   455 3611

Deli/grocery/wines, etc.

New York Bagel Bar
Knightsbridge Station (Brompton Road entrance), SW1

Sells bagels and latkes.

Nosha's Deli
629 Watford Way, NW7   959 4842

Noshers
429 Kingsbury Road, NW9   204 4197

Delicatessen; also does outside catering.

Panzer Delicatessen Ltd
13–19 Circus Road, NW8   722 8596 and 722 8162

Stocks wide range of kosher products, including smoked salmon, Grodzinski cakes and biscuits, new green cucumbers, Hebrew National meats, salami and canned soups, kosher wines, ice cream, pies and toppings. Freezer section.

Pelter Stores
82 Edgware Way, Edgware, Middx   958 6910

'Heimische' speciality foods, eg gefilte fish, schmaltz herrings from Gan Eden, stuffed carp, smoked salmon, salads, etc. Israeli frozen products, kosher pre-packed meats.

Platters
10 Halleswelle Parade, Finchley Road, NW11   455 7345

Grocers/deli.

Rogg's
137 Cannon Street Road, E1   488 3368

Delicatessen. Herrrings and cucumbers pickled on the premises.

Sabra's Delicatessen
119 The Broadway, NW7   906 1132

Large selection of Israeli wines. Take-away section includes sandwiches, hot cutlets, latkes, salads, salt beef, salami, egg and onion, chopped herring, cakes, also hot coffee. Deli sells everything from salmon and gefilte fish to rye bread and cholla.

Safeways
Supermarket chain. Branches stocking kosher foods include Barbican, Blackheath, Bloomsbury, Chelsea, Ealing, East Sheen, Edgware Road, Hammersmith, Holloway, Kensington, Lewisham, South Norwood, Stamford Hill, Streatham, Sydenham, Upper Norwood, Wembley, Wimbledon.

Sainsbury's
Supermarket chain. Branches stocking kosher food include Cromwell Road, Nine Elms, Finchley Road (particularly large selection).

Sammy's Delicatessen
17 Edgwarebury Lane, Edgware, Middx   958 3178

Worsht, viennas, potato latkes, salmon rissoles, etc.

Selfridges Food Hall
400 Oxford Street, W1   629 1234

Has a large kosher section, selling pre-packed meats, fish, cheese, frozen latkes, bagels, pizzas, pies, ice cream, canned groceries, biscuits, ready meals, desserts, and assorted pickled cucumbers. Enormous selection of kosher wines. Will even do a 'Jewish hamper for Christmas'!

Tesco
Supermarket chain. The following branches stock kosher foods: Bethnal Green, Borehamwood, Finchley Central (which even has gefilte fish on the deli counter), Goodge Street, Harrow, South Tottenham, Hendon, Ilford.

Waitrose
Supermarket chain. Range of kosher foods available at branches in Kenton, Temple Fortune, Enfield, Brent Cross and Finchley Road.

Kosher Butchers and Poulterers

The following kosher butchers and poulterers are licensed by the London Board for Shechita, 1 Bridge Lane, Finchley Road, NW11, 458 8399. This board was established in 1804 to administer the affairs of Shechita in London.

Butchers which are licensed by the Kedassia, the Joint Kashrus Committee of the Union of Orthodox Hebrew Congregations, the Adath Yisroel Synagogue and the Golders Green Beth Hamedrash Congregation are listed on page 75.

KOSHER BUTCHERS

L. Botchin
94 St John's Wood High Street, NW8   722 4616

A. Cohen
5 The Broadway, Wembley, Middx   904 2662 and 904 7625

M. Cohen
4 Cat Hill, East Barnet, Herts   449 9215

N. L. Cohen
563 Kingsbury Road, NW9   204 8649

S. Cohen
20 Ashfield Parade, N14   886 9810

S. Cohen
93b Upper Clapton Road, E5   806 5035

P. Evans
292 Stamford Hill, N16   800 3816

H. Friend
83 Stanmore Hill, Stanmore, Middx   954 0820

K. Gamse
423 Kingsbury Road, NW9   204 2238

H. Gitlin
3 Walm Lane, NW2   459 5344

J. Glass
7 Ridley Road, E8   254 7612

N. Goldberg
12 Claybury Broadway, Redbridge, Ilford, Essex   551 2828

B. Green
86a Hamlets Way, E3   980 2963

S. Greenspan
9–11 Lyttelton Road, N2   455 9921 and 455 7709

B. Gross (Machzike Hadath)
6 Russell Parade, Golders Green Road, NW11   455 6662 and
455 6663

P. Herskine
7 Beehive Lane, Ilford, Essex   554 3238

Mrs R. Ismach
230 Regents Park Road, N3   346 6554

P. M. Joseph
83a Fairfax Road, NW6   624 5527

A. Kaye
8 Amhurst Parade, N16   800 5520

Mrs D. Kaye
12a Highview Parade, Ilford, Essex   550 9717

L. Kelman
198 Preston Road, Wembley, Middx   904 0897

D. Kreeger
25 Station Parade, Cockfosters, N14   449 9124

Mrs R. Lewin
18e Manor Road, N16   802 7976

E. Lion
145 Clarence Road, E5   985 6989

M. Lipowcz
9 Royal Parade, Ealing, W5   567 7184

J. Lyons
2 Cazenove Road, N16   254 3535

H. Malka
61 Brent Street, NW4   202 8758

Mrs A. Mann
23 Edgwarebury Lane, Edgware, Middx   958 3789

L. Mann
35 Vivian Avenue, NW4   202 5252

R. Markovitch
371 Edgware Road, W2   723 4633

A. Perlmutter
162 Bowes Road, N11   888 1693

G. Rees
10 Empire Way, Wembley, Middx   902 0058

J. Robotkin
417 Hendon Way, NW4   202 9801

E. Samiloff
8 Onslow Parade, N14   368 4265

E. Samiloff
53 Shenley Road, Borehamwood, Herts   207 2858 and
207 2782

S. Samuels
30 Red Lion Street, Richmond, Surrey   940 3060 and
940 6282

J. Schlagman
37 Aylmer Parade, East Finchley, N2   340 6550

L. Schlagman
112 Regents Park Road, N3   346 3598

Mrs B. Shaw
49 Streatham Hill, SW2   674 6763 and 674 3626

H. G. Shovel
233 Lower Clapton Road, E5   985 8053

I. Silverman
4 Canons Corner, Stanmore, Middx   958 8682

L. S. Simons
720 Eastern Avenue, Newbury Park, Essex   518 0968

M. Szwarc
84 Edgware Way, Edgware, Middx   958 8454 and 958 6557

S. Waldman
10 Crescent Road, E6   472 0735

I. Zell
212 Jubilee Street, E1   790 3810

KOSHER POULTERERS

J. Alter
1a Downs Court Parade, E8   985 7803

V. Charing
132 Ridley Road, E8   254 2735

E. Gold
222 Jubilee Street, E1   790 1572

H. Kaye
1029 Finchley Road, NW11   455 3286

P. Lipman
36 Hessel Street, E1   480 5741

L. Minster
141 Hale Lane, Edgware, Middx   959 6068

C. Solomons
646 Cranbrook Road, Ilford, Essex   554 6562

P. R. Solomons (stall)
Goulston Street, E1

The following butchers are licensed by the Kedassia, the Joint Kashrus Committee of the Union of Orthodox Hebrew Congregations, the Adath Yisroel Synagogue and the Golders Green Beth Hamedrash Congregation.

KOSHER BUTCHERS

Edgware Kosher Butchers
9 Whitchurch Parade, Edgware, Middx   952 2574 and 952 5887

E. & F. Ltd
99 Upper Clapton Road, E5   806 5360

F. Frohwein & Sons Ltd
1097 Finchley Road, NW11   455 9848 and 455 1914

F. Frompack (London) Ltd
70 Stamford Hill, N16   806 7866

Hendon Kosher Food Stores Ltd
9–11 Watford Way, NW4   202 4471

M. Rosenbaum
166 Stamford Hill, N16   800 2506

Books and Judaica Specialists

Whether you're interested in books by Jewish authors or works on Jewish subjects, in history or religion, you'll find no shortage of helpful and well-stocked shops and book departments in London.

Many of the specialist shops also sell Jewish items such as menorot (candlesticks), kipot (skull-caps) and other religious articles.

Aisenthal
11 Ashbourne Parade, Finchley Road, NW11   455 0501
Mon–Thurs 9 am–6 pm   Fri 9 am–4 pm (summer)   9 am–2 pm (winter)   Sun 9.30 am–1.30 pm

Stocks Hebraic and English books of Jewish interest. Also traditional gifts, cassettes, children's books and novelty toys.

The Alternative Bookshop
3 Langley Court, Covent Garden, WC2   240 1804
Mon–Sat 11 am–6 pm

Political bookshop specializing in 'free market economics', with a strong interest in Jewish affairs. Has a selection of pro-Zionist and pro-Israel literature and books on general Jewish history and Middle East politics. Hold regular book-signing sessions, which have included books of Jewish interest, as well as seminars. You can write for a free events list and to be put on their mailing lists.

Blue and White Shop
6 Beehive Lane, Ilford, Essex   518 1982
Mon–Wed 9 am–5.30 pm   Thurs 9 am–3 pm   Fri 9 am–1 pm Sun 9 am–1.15 pm

Wide selection of Jewish books on history, prayer, Israel, theology, novels. Also menorot, Israeli glassware, records, tapes, greetings cards and religious requisites.

Carmel Gifts
62 Edgware Way, Edgware, Middx   958 7632
Mon–Thurs 9 am–5.30 pm   Fri 9 am–3 pm   Sun 9 am–1.30 pm

As well as a large selection of books for both adults and children, also stocks greetings cards, mezuzot (scrolls), menorot, and other religious articles and gifts. Selection of Jewish calendars, also wrapping paper, etc.

Faculty Books
98 Ballards Lane, Finchley, N3   346 7761 and 346 0145
Mon–Sat 9.30 am–5.30 pm

Large selection of books of Jewish interest, with subjects ranging from philosophy to memoirs.

Fagins Books Ltd
62 Chase Side, Southgate, N14   882 5690
Mon–Fri 9.30 am–5.30 pm   Sat 9 am–5.30 pm

Small section of Jewish books, including Jewish cookery books.

R. Golub & Co Ltd
27 Osborn Street, E1   247 7430
Mon–Thurs 10 am–5 pm   Fri and Sun 10 am–1 pm

Large shop known as 'the Jewish bookshop of the East End'. Stocks books in both Hebrew and English. Wide selection of Judaica, Hebraica and religious requisites. Wholesale and retail. Mail order available.

Hatchards
187 Piccadilly, W1   439 9921
Mon–Fri 9 am–5.30 pm   Sat 9 am–5 pm

Has a small selection of books of Jewish interest. Hatchards say they 'will obtain any British book in print'.

The Hebrew Book and Gift Centre
18 Cazenove Road, N16   254 3963
Mon–Thurs 10 am–6.30 pm   Early closing Fri   Sun 10 am–3 pm

Stocks religious books in both Hebrew and English, as well as gifts including menorot and ritual gifts, records and tapes.

Henry Pordes Books Ltd
58–60 Charing Cross Road, WC2   836 9031
Mon–Sat 10 am–7 pm

Has a large section of second-hand Judaica. Also Middle East plate books and other rare Judaica.

B. Hirschler
62 Portland Avenue, N16   800 6395

Specialist in rare second-hand Jewish books. Phone for appointment.

Jerusalem The Golden
146a Golders Green Road, NW11   455 4960 and 458 7011
Mon–Thurs 9.30 am–6 pm   Fri 9.30 am–4 pm   Sun 10 am–2 pm

Specialists in Judaica and Hebraica. Also stocks all Jewish religious items, Israeli handicraft gifts. Has a large record section including Jewish cantorial and Hebrew.

Jewish Chronicle Bookshop
25 Furnival Street, EC4   405 9252
Mon–Thurs 9.30 am–5 pm   Fri 9.30 am–3 pm

Has a wide selection of books for all the family on subjects from cookery to children's Hebrew dictionaries, from Chasidic through to Jewish feminism. Many book sets suitable for bar-mitzvah presents. Mail order available.

Jewish Memorial Council Bookshop
Woburn House, Upper Woburn Place, WC1   387 3081
Mon–Thurs 10 am–5.30 pm   Fri 10 am–2 pm (winter) and
10 am–4 pm (summer)   Sun 10.30 am–12.45 pm

General Jewish bookshop with books on Judaism, Israel, bibles, biographies, etc. Good selection of Hebrew and Yiddish dictionaries. Also sells religious artefacts and greetings cards.

Lawrence Cohen Books
297 Hale Lane, Edgware, Middx   958 6677
Mon–Sat 9.30 am–5.30 pm   Sun 10 am–1 pm

General bookshop with Jewish leanings. Strongest on literature and general Judaica side rather than on religious books. Titles range from novels by Bernice Rubens and Isaac Bashevis Singer to works on the history and philosophy of Judaism. Holds a Jewish Book Week at a local synagogue every year – usually Stanmore United or Edgware Reform.

Manor House Books
80 East End Road, N3   346 2288 and 445 4293
Mon–Thurs 10 am–4 pm   Fri, Sun 10 am–1 pm

Large selection of Judaica and Hebraica – around 2,000 books, both new and second-hand. Also bargain books, children's books, gifts, cards, antique prints and maps.

Menorah Print and Gift Shop
227 Golders Green Road, NW11   458 8289
Mon–Thurs 9.30 am–1 pm   2 pm–6 pm   Fri 9.30 am–1 pm
Sun 9.45 am–1 pm

Stocks religious books in Hebrew and English as well as embroidery and silverware gifts.

Selfridges
400 Oxford Street, W1   629 1234
Mon–Sat 9 am–5.30 pm   Thurs 9 am–7 pm

Has a large section devoted to Jewish books in the Book Department on the fourth floor. Sells an extensive range of gifts and Jewish religious items, including menorot and kipot. Also barmitzvah cards, Jewish New Year cards and other Jewish greetings cards in the Stationery Department.

Stamford Hill Stationers
153 Clapton Common, E5   802 5222
Mon–Thurs 9 am–5 pm   Fri 9 am–¾ hour before Shabbat
Sun 9 am–1 pm

Selection of books of general Jewish interest plus a full range of prayer-books. Also gifts such as ashtrays, barmitzvah presents, menorot, tefilin, mezuzot, etc.

Banks

The following Israeli banks have branches in London.

Bank Hapoalim
West End: 8–12 Brook Street, W1   499 0792
City: Princes House, 95 Gresham Street, EC2   600 0382

West End branch is open 9.15 am–3.30 pm Mon–Fri; City Branch 9.15 am–3 pm Mon–Fri.

Bank Leumi
Head Office/West End branch: 4–7 Woodstock Street, W1   629 1205

City: Swan House, 34–35 Queen Street, EC4   248 7712

Suburban branches:
242 Station Road, Edgware, Middx   958 1166
380–382 Cranbrook Road, Gants Hill, Ilford, Essex   554 8217
99–101 Golders Green Road, NW11   458 9311

Suburban branches are open from 9.30 am–4.15 pm (closed Shabbat), and 10 am–12.30 pm on Sundays. The West End and City branches are open from 9.30 am–3.45 pm Mon–Fri.

Synagogues

There are over 160 Jewish congregations in and around London, so wherever you are staying you should find a place of worship within walking distance. Visitors are always welcome at services.

Many synagogues are of particular historical and architectural interest, and some give guided tours of their buildings. On the following pages you will find detailed information on a selection of London's synagogues.

Many synagogues have social committees and help Jewish families make new friends in the area; some have communal meals after services; most publish a synagogue magazine or newsletter giving details of local activities.

The synagogue office will give details of services, times when it would be convenient to look around the building, information on the social activities of the community, etc, as well as general local information. (NB: If telephoning from outside the London area, dial 01 before the number.)

My thanks to all the synagogues who helped me compile the section on interesting communities in different areas of London. A full directory of synagogues in and around London appears on pages 112–118.

The Main Synagogue Movements

UNITED SYNAGOGUE

Five synagogues, the oldest of which is known as 'The Great Synagogue' and dates back to the 16th century, amalgamated in 1870 to form the United Synagogue.

Solomon Hirschell, the Rabbi of the Great Synagogue, was recognized in 1808 as the 'Presiding Rabbi' of the three founder City synagogues of the Ashkenazi community – the Great Synagogue in Duke's Place, which was destroyed in the Second World War and moved to Adler House, Adler Street, E1, where

the congregation worshipped until the closure of the synagogue in 1977; the Hambro' Synagogue in Fenchurch Street, EC3 (established in 1707 and closed in 1936), and the New Synagogue in Leadenhall Street, EC3 (established in 1761 and now situated in Stamford Hill, N16). From his office developed that of the Chief Rabbi of the United Hebrew Congregations of the British Commonwealth.

Today the United Synagogue comprises both constituent and affiliated synagogues, and provides religious facilities for over 40,000 Orthodox Ashkenazi families. It is also responsible for a great deal of social and philanthropic work in the community, its committees dealing with everything from youth services to the supervision of kashrus. It also has a Burial Society.

FEDERATION OF SYNAGOGUES

A number of small and homely synagogues were set up in East London by European immigrants, and 16 of these amalgamated in 1887 to form the Federation of Synagogues.

Federation East London synagogues included Bethnal Green Great, Commercial Road Great, Canon Street Road, New Road and Philpot Street synagogues. Today the Federation of Synagogues has constituent synagogues and affiliated congregations all over London.

Associated bodies include the Office of the Rav Rashi, the Beth Din of the Federation of Synagogues, the London Kashrus Board, the London Talmud Torah Council and the Federation Burial Society.

UNION OF ORTHODOX HEBREW CONGREGATIONS

This was founded in 1926 by the late Rabbi Dr V. Shonfeld to protect traditional Judaism. It consists of bodies affiliated to the Adath Yisroel Burial Society and others who want to protect Orthodoxy. In addition to the constituent synagogues, the Union comprises direct membership as laid down in the Constitution.

Membership of the Union synagogues is over 6,000.

INDEPENDENT SYNAGOGUES

These are independent congregations, each following its own code of practice. A selection of their philosophies and histories can be found on the following pages.

SEPHARDI

The Spanish and Portuguese Jews' Community was founded in London in the 17th century. The congregation worshipped in Creechurch Lane, EC3, until Bevis Marks, London's first synagogue, was built in 1701 (see pages 8 and 157).

This community has two other constituent synagogues: in Maida Vale (dating from 1896), and Wembley (opened in 1977).

The congregation is run by a Board of Elders and an Executive of five members. Institutions connected with the Spanish and Portuguese Congregation include a Burial Society, Welfare Board, the Sephardi Kashrut Authority, a Communal Centre and a Home for the Aged.

There are also a number of other Sephardi synagogues, for Eastern Jewry, Persian Jews, etc (see Synagogue Directory, pages 112–118).

REFORM SYNAGOGUES OF GREAT BRITAIN

The Reform Synagogues of Great Britain came into being in 1840. Its aims were to establish a synagogue 'where a revised service may be performed at hours more suited to our habits and . in a manner more calculated to inspire feelings of devotion, where religious instruction may be afforded by competent persons and where, to effect these purposes, Jews generally may form a united congregation under the denomination of British Jews'. (See West London Synagogue of British Jews, West London/West End section.)

Women are afforded equal membership status in these synagogues and can hold all synagogue offices. Members are also permitted to travel by car or public transport to services on Shabbat.

UNION OF LIBERAL AND PROGRESSIVE SYNAGOGUES

Liberal Judaism is 'traditional Judaism brought up-to-date, and is an attempt to revive the creativity that has always characterized Judaism during its periods of dynamic growth and development. It combines respect for Jewish tradition with a frank acceptance of modern knowledge and due regard for the realities of the world in which we live.

'It stresses ethics more than ritual, affirms the freedom and responsibility of the individual to act in accordance with his conscience, and accords men and women equal status in the synagogue in marriage law.'

The oldest Liberal synagogue dates back to 1912 (see The Liberal Jewish Synagogue, North London/North-West London section).

North London/North-West London

UNITED SYNAGOGUE

Bushey and District Synagogue
177–189 Sparrows Herne, Bushey Heath, Herts   950 7340

A modern, multi-purpose building consecrated on 28 April 1985. The synagogue organizes a number of social events, from a friendship club for the over 55s to Israeli dancing. Details from the synagogue office.

Cockfosters & North Southgate Synagogue
Old Farm Avenue, N14   886 8225

A traditional synagogue built in 1952, with a communal hall and classroom extension built in 1964. The synagogue has 10 beautiful stained-glass windows. The community holds a number of social events, such as yoga classes, as well as 'Project Seed' adult education classes which cover subjects such as reading Hebrew, a woman's role in Judaism, how to conduct a Seder Service. Details from the synagogue office between 10 am–12.30 pm Sun–Fri, 1.30 pm–4 pm Tuesday.

Cricklewood Synagogue
131 Walm Lane, NW2   452 1739

Fifty years old, this synagogue has beautiful stained-glass windows by the artist David Hillman.

Edgware Synagogue
Edgware Way, Edgware, Middx   958 7508

A traditional-style building erected around 35 years ago, with internal stained-glass windows. Visitors are welcome – contact the synagogue office for an appointment. The secretary will also be able to give details of clubs, etc. An Orthodox synagogue, with services organized on traditional lines.

Hampstead Garden Suburb Synagogue
Norrice Lea, Lyttelton Road, N2   455 8126

This synagogue was founded in 1934 and the present neo-Georgian building was erected in 1958. Visitors are welcome to visit by appointment. A number of social activities are offered, including a drama group and an over-50s club. Full details on request.

Hornsey & Wood Green (Affiliated) Synagogue
Wightman Road, N8   (No telephone)

This synagogue was rebuilt in 1959 as a hall with the end portion consecrated with the Ark. Since there is only a small and declining congregation, the only activity is synagogue service: open every Sabbath and Yomtov only.

Mill Hill Synagogue
Station Road, Mill Hill, NW7   959 1137

A modern synagogue built in 1960. Communal activities include a bridge club, 'Project Seed' adult education, etc. Full details from the synagogue office.

Muswell Hill Synagogue
31 Tetherdown, N10   883 5925

A modern building erected in 1965 with a Holocaust Memorial Window designed by Britain's first official War Office Poster Designer, Abram Games, who was famous for his controversial 'Your talk may kill' warning poster. Visiting (on Sunday mornings) by appointment. The synagogue has social committees, a friendship club, etc. Details on request from the secretary.

New Synagogue
Egerton Road, N16   800 6003 (10 am–12.30 pm)

This synagogue is of traditional design, with beautiful stained-glass windows replaced after bombing during the Second World War. The synagogue was originally built in 1838 in Great St Helens, Bishopsgate, and transferred to Stamford Hill in 1915. The Ark and lamps on the Bima are the originals, as are curtains and silverware. The Chief Rabbi, Sir Immanuel Jakobovits, worshipped here as a young man. Appointments to visit should be made with the secretary.

Palmers Green & Southgate Synagogue
Brownlow Road, N11   881 0037
(Office open Sundays 10 am–12 noon)

A modern building with many stained-glass windows, some lit by natural daylight and others with fluorescent back-lighting. It was erected in the 1930s, bombed during 1940, and rebuilt after the War. The building was also extended, modernized, and the first-floor hall and facilities added in 1977. Congregants include past mayors of the Boroughs of Southgate and Enfield.

The synagogue holds a friendship club for the over 60s and a SPEC Jewish Youth and Community Centre is nearby. Rabbi Joseph Shaw would be able to introduce Jewish visitors to local families.

St John's Wood Synagogue
37–41 Grove End Road, NW8   286 3838 and 286 6333

This synagogue is one of the largest in the country; the design is modern and the stained-glass windows are by the artist David Hillman.

The present synagogue building was erected in 1964 but the congregation itself began in 1876 and the Abbey Road Synagogue consecrated in 1882. St John's Wood Synagogue was the first synagogue to be founded under the auspices of the United Synagogue.

The synagogue's facilities are often used for international conferences, and the building has a regular stream of visitors from all over the world.

The synagogue office is happy to provide a list of activities and/or arrange hospitality or meals for visitors. Non-Jewish visitors are advised to notify their attendance at services in advance so that they may be seated beside a congregant who will explain the service to them.

Woodside Park Synagogue
Woodside Park Road, N12   445 4236

This synagogue has just been rebuilt and was consecrated by the Chief Rabbi on 6 April 1986. It has several stained-glass windows taken from South-East London Synagogue.

The exquisite Ark and Bima were built in the 1930s in Sunderland, Tyne and Wear, and have been reinstalled and redesigned in this building. Visitors will be welcome by appointment.

FEDERATION

Machzike Hadath Synagogue
3 Highfield Road, Golders Green, NW11   455 9816

A strictly Orthodox purpose-built synagogue consecrated on 4 September 1983, just before Rosh Hashana 5744. It has 12 stained-glass windows. All the pews were made in Kibbutz Lavi in Israel, as were a number of other items. Part of the roof can be opened for chuppot.

The synagogue was originally in East London, and known as Spitalfields Great Synagogue, the Machzike Hadath community coming into existence in 1891 at a time when religious observance in Britain was in decline. The synagogue soon became one of the most important Orthodox congregations in Great Britain, and was recognized as the focal point of Orthodox Jewish practice and learning.

This position in the Jewish community was attained under the leadership of such eminent Rabbinic personalities as Rabbi Aba Werner, Rabbi A. I. Kook (later Chief Rabbi of Israel), Rabbi Y. Abramsky and, more recently, Rabbi Simcha Lopian.

The community flourished up to the outbreak of hostilities in 1939 but during and after the War most of the Jewish residents moved away from the East End to other parts of London. In 1948 the Machzike Hadath acquired a site at the corner of Bridge Lane and North Circular Road with the intention of building a new synagogue there. Planning permission was, however, revoked because of a proposed road-widening scheme, and for 26 years regular services were held at the private residence of the late Rabbi Lopian in Golders Green.

The foundation stone of the new synagogue in Highfield Road was laid on 17 January 1982. The Chief Rabbi, Sir Immanuel Jakobovits, was unable to attend as he was abroad, but he wrote a letter which was read out on the occasion. In it he said: 'The rebirth of the Machzike Hadath Synagogue brings back particularly precious personal memories to me. Not only did I frequently worship at the Machzike Hadath in Brick Lane in the late 1940s, especially during my ministry at Duke's Place, but I was on several occasions privileged to deliver a sermon to what was then indeed a "Torah fortress in Anglo-Jewry".'

Visitors are asked to telephone between 10 am–12 noon on Sundays for an appointment; they are also welcome at shiurim.

UNION OF ORTHODOX HEBREW CONGREGATIONS

Adath Yisroel Synagogue
40 Queen Elizabeth's Walk, N16   802 6262

A modern, traditionally-designed building, built in 1954, with an adjacent mikva (ritual bath) for ladies. The synagogue is strictly Orthodox and is also the parent synagogue for many other Orthodox synagogues.

Visitors should make an appointment with the beadle or secretary, who could also put them in touch with other Jewish families.

Hendon Adath Yisroel Congregation
11 Brent Street, NW4   202 9183

An Orthodox synagogue, built in 1948 and rebuilt in 1958. It has beautiful stained-glass windows. Visitors should make an appointment with the secretary.

On Sabbaths and festivals visitors are only admitted if they conform to strictly Orthodox Jewish practice and observance. If in doubt about what this entails, visitors should consult the secretary in advance.

North Hendon Adath Yisroel Synagogue
Holders Hill Road, NW4   203 2390 (secretary 203 0797)

A modern building with stained-glass windows – on the ground floor these depict the Sabbath and festivals, and on the first floor the 12 tribes of Israel.

The synagogue was founded in 1948, at which time it used the premises of the Hasmonean School. The present building was opened in September 1965. Visits are only permitted during service times, and women are reminded that they must cover their heads.

An Orthodox synagogue, the services are conducted in the Ashkenazi pronunciation. There is also a daily 'Daf Yomi' lecture★ given by the Rabbi, Rabbi D. Cooper, as well as other lectures on Talmud.

★ These lectures take place all over the world, so that when visiting another town or country men can keep up with their study of the Talmud. Many Orthodox synagogues have similar lectures.

INDEPENDENT SYNAGOGUES

New London Synagogue

33 Abbey Road, St John's Wood, NW8   328 1026

The New London Synagogue was born at a meeting in a Kensington hotel on 3 May 1964 – the child of a controversy that none of its founders had sought.

Rabbi Dr Louis Jacobs was minister of the New West End Synagogue from 1954–59. In that period, through his preaching and his writings, he propounded a philosophy of religious Judaism which he was later to sum up in these words:

'We can no longer accept the view that Jewish thought is simply a question of trust, automatic and static transmission of our religious tradition. We must take into account all the influence which time and environment have brought to bear upon this tradition . . .'

Rabbi Dr Jacobs resigned from the New West End Synagogue in 1959 to take up an appointment at Jews' College. But when, in 1961, he was recommended to be appointed as Principal of the college, the then Chief Rabbi, Israel Brodie, pronounced himself 'unable to accept the recommendation'.

Shortly afterwards, Rabbi Dr Jacobs resigned from Jews' College, as did a number of the lay members of its Council who had supported his candidature as Principal.

When, in February 1964, the pulpit at the New West End Synagogue again became vacant, the board of management and a selection committee unanimously recommended that Rabbi Dr Jacobs should be recalled to his former position. But again the Chief Rabbi refused to give his approval.

The New West End Synagogue, however, would not accept the ban and, acting in the belief that the attitude of the Chief Rabbi was devoid of any justification, it came to the conclusion that there was no alternative but to resist it.

On 18 April 1964, on the invitation of the board of management, Rabbi Dr Jacobs returned to the pulpit of the New West End Synagogue. Five days later, at a meeting of the Council of the United Synagogue, the honorary officers and board of management of the New West End Synagogue were dismissed and four 'managers' appointed in their place.

On 3 May 1964 the meeting of members of the New West End Synagogue resolved upon the establishment of the New London

Synagogue, and six days later members of the New London Synagogue worshipped together for the first time.

On 29 August 1964 the congregation met for the first time in its own building in Abbey Road, St John's Wood. A week later, on the first day of Rosh Hashana, Rabbi Dr Jacobs in his sermon reviewed the terms used to describe the New London Synagogue 'an independent Orthodox congregation'.

It was independent, he said, because 'we have decided to take our destiny into our own hands, to work it out for ourselves . . .' And it was Orthodox, he said, because the congregation believed in God, the Torah and Israel.

'The New London,' says Rabbi Dr Jacobs, 'is traditional in its services, in its attitude towards the Sabbath and the dietary laws, and in its respect for the values of the past.'

The synagogue is as near as one can get to the American Conservative Synagogues, except that at statutory services men and women do not sit together.

Social activities include a single and married group for ages 21–35 which meets once a month.

New North London Synagogue
The Manor House, 80 East End Road, N3   346 8560

This synagogue was founded on 3 November 1974, when it was resolved 'to constitute an independent congregation for the advancement and promotion of the practice and teaching of traditional Judaism.'

Its objectives are: 'to be a synagogue which is a real community, where traditional Judaism is taught and practised in a way which is intellectually honest and satisfying to its members, which is independent of outside control, and which will provide all communal necessities including education, study groups, communal welfare, marriages and a burial scheme.'

The synagogue's theology is based on the teachings of Rabbi Dr Louis Jacobs (see New London Synagogue, above) and although it regards itself as a child of New London Synagogue, it has been independently constituted and its aims are 'to grow into a flourishing and worthy partner of our parent synagogue.

'Within the Anglo-Jewish community our function is to offer traditional Judaism which does not involve acceptance of untenable ideas. We will do our best to avoid controversy and our long-term aim is to build a bridge within the community and not to create another division.'

The community is self-sufficient, relying on its members for the performance of religious and other functions, in which all are encouraged to participate. Women have individual membership status and are eligible for election to all offices.

The synagogue is a lofty, spacious and peaceful room, originally the chapel of Finchley Manor House, its main feature being the curtains of the Ark.

Details of clubs, etc, available from the secretary.

SEPHARDI

Jacob Benjamin Elias Synagogue
140 Stamford Hill, N16

Ohel David Eastern Synagogue
Broadwalk Lane, Golders Green, NW11
(also **Eastern Jewry Synagogue**
Station Hall, Newbury Park, Ilford, Essex)   806 8109

The synagogue in Stamford Hill was established in 1958, in Golders Green in 1968, and in Ilford in 1975. They serve the Eastern Jewry community.

Visiting is by appointment only. Contact Mr D. Elias, the Hon Secretary of the three synagogues, during office hours, Mon–Thurs 10 am–1 pm. Their Sefer Torahs are ancient and particularly beautiful, and, says Mr Elias, they would be happy to show them to interested visitors.

REFORM

Edgware and District Reform Synagogue
118 Stonegrove, Edgware, Middx   958 9782

This congregation was founded in 1935 by a small group of stalwarts who met in rented halls and private houses. At that time, although Reform had existed in Britain since 1840, it had expanded little and only three congregations existed.

Edgware was one of the first of the new Reform congregations to be founded in the suburbs to which Jews were then moving. It closed during the Second World War but restarted afterwards, and in 1948 Rabbi Dr I. Maybaum became its first Rabbi.

Edgware and District Reform Synagogue is now one of the largest synagogues within the R.S.G.B. Every Jewish person (ie one who is born of a Jewish mother or converted to Judaism according to their standards) is eligible for membership.

Despite the size of the congregation, they try, through meetings in members' houses (Chavurot), to improve personal contact. They have smaller groups for religious and social gatherings, which also serve the purpose of creating ways to meet the rabbis. From time to time they have communal Sabbath Eve meals together with an Oneg held at the synagogue.

Among the synagogue's activities are a Shul Shuttle – a minicab service for people with no means of transport to services (the synagogue accepts that in our time transport may be used to attend both Friday and Saturday Sabbath services) – a library, a youth centre, an association for Jewish one-parent families, and a music group.

The synagogue was built in 1955 and an administration block added in 1965.

Hampstead Reform Jewish Community
56 Lymington Road, NW6   485 6726

This community is in a Borough of Camden 'short-life' building where some services are held; others are held in members' homes or at Friends' House, Heath Street, Hampstead, NW3. The community was founded in 1975 and further information can be obtained from Andy Becker on the above number.

Middlesex New Synagogue
39 Bessborough Road, Harrow, Middx   864 0133

A modern synagogue which was completed in 1977, although the community has been in existence for over 25 years. Famous members have included Emma Samms of 'Dynasty' fame.

Visitors wishing to meet local Jewish families or learn about clubs, etc, should contact either the Rabbi or the Administrator at the synagogue.

North-Western Reform Synagogue
Alyth Gardens, NW11   455 6763

This synagogue was originally founded in 1933, and its earliest services were held in a private home near Golders Green. Temporary quarters were then the small Hawthorn Hall, where the religion classes met; and the first High Festival services were held in the Hampstead Garden Suburb Centre. A choir was assembled and a small pipe-organ acquired.

Membership grew slowly but steadily, and from the start it was evident that a growing number of Jews who had fled from Germany and settled in the area gravitated towards 'Alyth'. It is interesting to note that the architect of the synagogue's Sanctuary and the artist who designed the bronze plaque of the Ten Commandments over the entrance were both German refugees.

The existing synagogue was opened in 1935, and has recently-commissioned stained-glass windows designed and made by Roman Halter – the theme of which is 'The Celebration of Life', which Mr Halter describes as 'a gathering-together into 18 windows of visual images of parts of nature, views of Israel, of inscriptions, timeless and wise from our Bible.' There are also beautiful tapestry wall-hangings made by members of the congregation in honour of the synagogue's 50th anniversary.

Contact the synagogue office for details of social activities, clubs, etc.

Southgate Reform Synagogue
45 High Street, N14   882 6828

This community was established in 1961 and moved into its present building in 1981. Particularly interesting are the synagogue's modern sculptures, Ner Tamid by Sylvia Leibson, and Holocaust Memorial by Naomi Blake.

Visitors are welcome to see these during services, the times of which vary. Contact the secretary for full details.

LIBERAL

Belsize Square Synagogue
51 Belsize Square, NW3   794 3949

This community was founded in 1939 by refugees from the Continent, and services were originally held in hired rooms. The membership today stands at 1,200 persons, and is available to both men and women.

Encouraged and aided in its establishment by the Union of Liberal and Progressive Synagogues, it owes much to its first distinguished Chairman, the Hon Lily H. Montagu CBE (see West Central Liberal Synagogue, West London/West End section) and first ministers, Rabbi Dr Georg Salzberger and Cantor Magnus Davidsohn.

From small beginnings in a house in Swiss Cottage, the numerical strength grew until premises on Belsize Square were acquired in 1947 and subsequently developed.

Facilities include an Israel Travel Scholarship – an annual award – and an Israel Cultural Society which arranges lectures, films and discussions.

The type of service is described as 'conservative, faithfully preserving the 19th-century romantic tradition of synagogue music, with rabbi, cantor, choir and organist'. Youth services with a youth choir are also held.

Hertsmere Progressive Synagogue
High Street, Elstree, Herts   953 0958

The 100-year-old building was originally a school-house, which has been modernized internally. It is a Grade III listed building, historical details of which can be seen in a recent book on Old Elstree.

For details of activities in the local community, etc, contact the Hon Secretary, Mrs Palmer, on Radlett 4666.

The Liberal Jewish Synagogue
28 St John's Wood Road, NW8   286 5181

This congregation was founded in 1912, and the synagogue built in 1925 in what was then a strikingly modern style. The architect was Ernest Joseph and interesting features include the façade of Grecian columns, the large Ark of carved wood and the murals by William Utermohlen in the Montefiore Hall.

The synagogue was half-destroyed by enemy bombing in 1940 and was rebuilt after the War.

It is the oldest and largest Liberal synagogue in the country, and its founder-president was Bible scholar and philanthropist Claude Goldsmid Montefiore.

Visitors wishing to meet local Jewish families should contact the secretary or the rabbis, who will be able to give details of clubs, etc.

North London Progressive Synagogue
100 Amhurst Park, N16   800 8931 and 800 0416

This used to be a Welsh chapel, built around 100 years ago and purchased by the synagogue in 1954. Services are modern, with men and women sitting together.

A cultural society meets once a month, with a varied programme. There is also a ladies' guild and a youth group.

Onegs are held regularly following services, which have a chazan and a choir. Full details from the secretary.

Northwood and Pinner Liberal Synagogue
Oaklands Gate, Northwood, Middx   Northwood (65) 22592

This congregation was founded in 1966, and the synagogue built five years ago of modern design. The focal point is a 19th-century wooden Ark surround from Czechoslovakia, and there are a number of other items connected with that country.

The synagogue also has a good Jewish library and a small Jewish museum. Visitors should make an appointment with Rabbi A. Goldstein on Northwood (65) 22818.

Southgate Progressive Synagogue
75 Chase Road, N14   886 0977

A Liberal synagogue using both Hebrew and English in its services and with no discrimination between men and women. The synagogue was formed just after the Second World War and the existing synagogue building erected in 1960.

Home hospitality can be arranged for visitors, if sufficient notice is given, and details of this and other facilities can be obtained from the synagogue secretary.

Wembley Liberal Synagogue
326 Preston Road, Harrow, Middx   904 8581

This synagogue was opened in 1948 when the first minister was Rev Vivian Simmons. It is of modern design and has a Holocaust memorial plaque on one wall.

Visitors are welcome by appointment with the synagogue secretary, who will also advise of service times, etc.

The synagogue has nearly 1,000 members and has a successful religion school. Other activities include a music group and adult education lectures.

East London/East End/Essex

UNITED SYNAGOGUE

Barking and Becontree Synagogue
200 Becontree Avenue, Dagenham, Essex   590 2737

As its name implies, this synagogue was formed by the amalgamation of two neighbouring communities. The Barking Synagogue was formed in 1924, mainly by local businessmen. At around this time the Dagenham Estate was created. This was Britain's first experiment in town planning, an attempt by the London County Council to relieve the overcrowding of the East and South-East of London. Not surprisingly, a few Jewish families were among those who came to live in the area.

In 1926, the Becontree and District Associate Synagogue was formed. The community comprised around 40 families and initially services were held in schools, church halls, co-op halls and other venues. By 1927 the number of families had grown to 120 and a suitable site was secured for a synagogue to serve the districts of Romford, Chadwell Heath, Goodmayes, Dagenham, Seven Kings and Ilford. The synagogue was consecrated on 25 March 1928.

The community continued to prosper, but with the migration from the East End to Ilford and Gants Hill, the focal point of Jewish life in the area shifted northward. The establishment of the Federation Synagogue in Ilford, and later the Beehive Lane Synagogue (which was to become the largest Jewish community in Britain) and the community at Romford, severely restricted the growth potential of the Becontree community.

The Barking Synagogue was also experiencing growth problems and by this time no longer had permanent premises, so the two communities amalgamated in 1948. The building was improved and the synagogue reconsecrated on 5 September 1954. The building as it stands today was reconsecrated by the Chief Rabbi, Dr Immanuel Jakobovits, on 20 September 1970.

The synagogue has a Friendship Club for senior synagogue members.

Chigwell and Hainault Synagogue
Limes Avenue, Limes Farm, Chigwell, Essex   500 2451

A modern, multi-purpose building erected in 1976 to serve a community which grew out of the Hainault community.

They would be happy to welcome guests, by arranging hospitality for Shabbat meals, for example. Contact the minister or the warden at the above address.

Wanstead and Woodford Synagogue
20 Churchfields, South Woodford, E18   530 3021

This synagogue was built in 1951 when building restrictions were in force, and there are therefore no special architectural features. Visitors who would like to see the synagogue should ring the above number in the evening for an appointment. Rabbi Saunders would be able to arrange for Jewish families to meet local families.

FEDERATION OF SYNAGOGUES

Congregation of Jacob
351–353 Commercial Road, Stepney, E1   550 8339 (secretary)

A traditional synagogue built in 1920 and bombed during the Second World War. Occasional Jewish tourists who have entered the synagogue have, says the secretary, been impressed at the efforts to keep it open despite the decline in the population of the area and the condition of the synagogue. The congregation runs a Chanucah Savings Club, the profits of which are put towards synagogue repairs and charity.

Great Garden Street Synagogue
7–9 Greatorex Street, E1   247 4436

This is a traditional Orthodox East End synagogue, around 80 years old, which fortunately suffered no war damage, unlike much of the area. The synagogue hall is home to a dairy restaurant (see Restaurant section) and the head office of the Federation of Synagogues has been built around the synagogue. Regretfully, says the secretary, the East End now offers nothing in the way of social facilities.

Ilford Federation Synagogue
14–16 Coventry Road, Ilford, Essex   554 5289

This synagogue was founded in 1931 but the present building – a beautiful, traditional synagogue with impressive stained-glass windows and a warm atmosphere – was consecrated in 1963.

An appointment to visit should be made with the secretary. The synagogue has a number of clubs for all ages, including a Friendship Club and a Yiddish Circle. It also provides a vast adult education network consisting of 25 weekly study sessions.

INDEPENDENT SYNAGOGUES

Sandy's Row Synagogue
4a Sandy's Row, Middlesex Street, E1   554 1078

This synagogue is situated in Spitalfields in the East End of London. It is one of Anglo-Jewry's oldest institutions, dating back to 1854. It was also the subject of a famous controversy . . .

The Dutch-Jewish immigrants who built the synagogue were poor people who had established what was essentially a working man's 'chevra', a pioneering effort which later developed into the Jewish friendly society.

They were mainly cigar-makers, diamond polishers and fruit tradesmen who had come to England to join relatives or improve their living conditions. At the time there were less than 20,000 Jews in London, and these immigrants brought to Whitechapel communal life a specific Dutch flavour.

Until 1854, when the foundations of Sandy's Row were laid, there were only three minor synagogues in East London, according to historian V. D. Lipman. These were the Rosemary Lane (Royal Mint Street) congregation founded in 1747, the Sun Square of Sun Yard 'Polish' synagogue established in 1792, and the Cutler Street 'Polish' synagogue founded about 1790. The designation 'Polish' apparently indicated the form of worship.

What is known today as Sandy's Row Synagogue was founded under the name 'Hevrath Menachem Avelim Hesed Ve'emeth', which is translated into English as 'Society of Kindness and Truth'. The name has its origins in the idea of a traditional burial, which is considered in Jewish tradition the truest form of kindness.

The society first used a small room in White's Row; later the Zetland Hall in Mansell Street was hired for festival services, and in 1867 a lease was taken of the French chapel in Artillery Lane, Bishopsgate.

By 1870 they had a regular synagogue with 500 members, known as the Parliament Square Congregation, but when the lease expired they had to raise £700 to extend it and repair the building, with the opportunity of enlarging it and making a new entrance from Sandy's Row. The congregation raised £200 and appealed to the community for the remainder.

This caused a great controversy: Lionel Louis Cohen, a Tory MP and the principal founder of the United Synagogue, argued that there was no need for a new congregation in Whitechapel which, he claimed, was ceasing to be a Jewish district. He suggested that the congregation should fill vacant seats in the City synagogues, which could be offered at reduced prices.

The pioneers of Sandy's Row argued that their synagogue fulfilled a vital need since it enabled persons of limited means to run their own congregation rather than becoming 'second-class members' of City houses of prayer.

The leaders of Sandy's Row Synagogue won the battle, and £350 was subscribed towards the total required. In an impressive ceremony, the synagogue was consecrated by the Haham, the very Rev Benjamin Artom. The Chief Rabbi, Dr Nathan Marcus Adler, declined the invitation because of the controversy relating to the amount of encouragement which should be given to small synagogues.

In 1887 Sandy's Row congregation became one of the 16 constituents of the Federation of Synagogues headed by Samuel Montagu, MP for Whitechapel and later Lord Swaythling, a prominent leader of the Chovovey Zion movement. His portrait still hangs in the boardroom of the synagogue.

In 1923 the congregation joined the United Synagogues as an Associated Synagogue and acquired the freehold of the property. But in 1949 it regained independence and since then has been associated for burial purposes with the West End Great Synagogue in Dean Street, W1.

SEPHARDI

Bevis Marks
St Mary Axe, EC3   626 1274

Britain's oldest synagogue, dating back to 1701 and still in use. Full details appear in London Landmarks, page 157.

Eastern Jewry Synagogue
Station Hall, Newbury Park, Ilford, Essex

Established in 1975. (See Sephardi section, North London/ North-West London.)

South London/Surrey

UNITED SYNAGOGUE

Catford & Bromley Synagogue
6 Crantock Road, Catford, SE6   698 3025

A modern building with beautiful stained-glass windows, this synagogue was founded in 1936 and the new synagogue building erected on its present site in 1969. Jewish families wishing to meet local families should contact Rabbi J. H. Rockman, telephone number above.

Richmond Synagogue

Until occupying their new synagogue in Lichfield Gardens, Richmond, in September 1986, this congregation will be located at temporary premises at the Vineyard School, Friar Styles Road, Richmond. Visitors are, however, welcome to attend services and activities.

Further details from the United Synagogue Head Office, Woburn House, Upper Woburn Place, WC1. Telephone 387 7891.

FEDERATION OF SYNAGOGUES

Woolwich & District
Anglesea Road, Woolwich, SE18   854 3188

The old Woolwich synagogue was established in 1900 but suffered bomb damage during the Second World War. It was rebuilt in 1962 and is therefore a modern-looking building.

Visitors wanting to see the synagogue should telephone the secretary, Mr J. M. Gaus, on 856 0845. He can also give details of the synagogue's friendship club, etc.

REFORM

Wimbledon & District Reform Synagogue
44–46 Worple Road, SW19   946 4836

A modern single-storey building built in 1951 for a congregation which was founded two years earlier. Offers a full calendar of social events as well as Shabbat and festival services, adult Hebrew classes, a friendship club, youth groups, Bible study classes, and a reference and lending library. Further details from the secretary.

LIBERAL

Kingston Liberal Synagogue
Rushett Road, Long Ditton, Surrey

A converted Victorian village school purchased by Kingston Liberal Synagogue in 1967. A new extension was added in 1984. Visitors wanting to visit the synagogue or meet other Jewish families are asked to write to the chairman, Gloria Ward, or secretary, Naomi Gould, at the above address.

South London Liberal Synagogue
1 Prentis Road, SW16   769 4787

This synagogue building, originally built in 1902 as a school hall, was acquired around 1938 and rebuilt in 1980. The congregation has one of Britain's best-known female rabbis – Rabbi Julia Neuberger – and is very liberal, offering an extremely warm and friendly atmosphere, especially on Friday nights. An interesting rabbi's chair from a synagogue at Kolin in Czechoslovakia can be seen when the synagogue is open for services.

Further details of this synagogue and its activities – which include socials such as whist drives – are obtainable from the secretary, telephone number above.

West London/West End

UNITED SYNAGOGUE

Central Synagogue
Great Portland Street, W1 (entrance in Hallam Street)
580 1355

This congregation was founded in 1855, its synagogue consecrated in 1870 and, unfortunately, destroyed in the Blitz in 1941. The new synagogue, a modern building of cantilever structure and with stained-glass windows depicting Jewish festivals, was consecrated in 1958. Visitors should make an appointment with the secretary between 10 am and 2 pm Monday–Thursday.

Ealing Synagogue
15 Grange Road, W5   998 1025 (secretary)

This synagogue was originally an old Victorian house which was enlarged before the Second World War and converted. The secretary could put you in touch with relevant clubs and groups, and visitors are welcomed by local families to Shabbat and Yomtov meals by prior arrangement.

Marble Arch Synagogue
32 Great Cumberland Place, W1   723 7246

A modern building erected in 1961 to replace the 'Great Synagogue' which was bombed during the Second World War. It has modern stained-glass windows. Visitors are welcome – appointments should be made with the secretary on the above telephone number.

FEDERATION OF SYNAGOGUES

Greenford Federation Synagogue
39–45 Oldfield Lane, South Greenford, Middx   578 2256

This community was founded immediately after the Second World War and the synagogue was opened in 1959. It is a modern brick building with a copper roof, and stained-glass windows comprising both modern and traditional designs.

The secretary points out that this synagogue has only a small, ageing and declining membership, with no resident minister, so that a minyan is only present on special occasions other than the main festivals. The shul is, however, open for Sabbath morning prayers.

There are no social clubs, but occasional Ladies' Guild functions.

Notting Hill Synagogue
206–208 Kensington Park Road, W11   952 4354 (secretary)

A traditional synagogue, built in 1900 and affiliated to the Federation of Synagogues. The building has just been reconsecrated, and although the community is ageing there are a number of younger members. Notting Hill is very near to the West End of London and visitors are welcome at the synagogue. The secretary will give details of visiting times.

INDEPENDENT SYNAGOGUES

West End Great Synagogue
21 Dean Street, W1   437 1873

The West End Great Synagogue comprises the several smaller congregations that used to exist around the West End of London. It is an independent community, with its own burial grounds in Streatham and Cheshunt.

The congregation was established and West End Talmud Torah founded at 10 Green's Court, W1, in 1880. In 1898 they held their first organized outing for children attending classes – it was to Chingford, and the price of 4d per head (around 1½p!) included tea.

The building fund started in 1899, with donations of £31.11s.9d (approximately £31.57p). The following year saw lectures by prominent Jews at the synagogue – these were advertized in *Jewish Telephone* at 1d (½p) per two lines.

In 1910 the synagogue amalgamated with Bikkur Cholim Synagogue, and premises were taken at 41 Brewer Street, W1. A burial ground at Streatham was purchased in 1914 to provide burial facilities for the West End Jewish populace, and this was consecrated the following year. (The other cemetery, at Cheshunt, was consecrated in 1968.)

In 1916 the West End Talmud Torah and Bikkur Cholim Synagogue moved to larger premises in Manette Street, W1, and were registered to comply with Civil Law as a House of Worship authorized to solemnize weddings; the first marriage was solemnized in the synagogue in 1917 at a cost of £1.11s.6d

(£1.55p), the couple being presented with silver candlesticks to mark the occasion.

A flag day was held in 1927 to raise money for the synagogue and the balance sheet, hitherto printed in Yiddish, was issued in English for the first time.

The synagogue moved to its present premises in Dean Street in 1941, and after amalgamating with Beth Hasepher in 1948 its name was changed to West End Great Synagogue. The synagogue suffered war damage and was reopened after some repairs were completed. The synagogue was rebuilt in 1960, reopened and consecrated in 1964.

The present modern building houses the synagogue, two large halls, the Ben Uri Art Gallery (see Sightseeing section), the synagogue offices, the offices of the burial society and the offices of Boys' Town Jerusalem, Labour Friends of Israel and British Na'amat.

As a community service, the synagogue has a stock of pre-cooked frozen meals which are available to visitors and others who may wish to eat. In cases of need the charges are reduced. In addition, the synagogue has recently allowed some students to occupy one of its flats, helping, in a small way, to alleviate the problem of student accommodation in London.

Visitors are welcome at services and the communal kiddush after each Sabbath and Festival morning service – full details from the synagogue office. The synagogue is also open for private prayer and shortly hopes to have a minyan each weekday morning.

SEPHARDI

Spanish & Portuguese Synagogue
8 St James's Gardens, W11   603 7961 and 603 3232

This is a Sephardi synagogue, most of its members originating from Greece and Turkey. An Oriental minhag (prayer custom) is kept, and the synagogue still holds a small number of services in Ladino Spanish.

The traditional synagogue was built in 1927 and visitors should make an appointment with the secretary.

REFORM

West London Synagogue of British Jews

34 Upper Berkeley Street, W1   723 4404

This congregation was founded in 1840 by Jewish families who lived in the fashionable West End of London. At that time the families concerned belonged to the synagogues in the East End of London, particularly to the Bevis Marks and Duke's Place synagogues, but it was a long and muddy walk on the Sabbath from the West to the East End of London.

It is also a Jewish custom that the synagogue should form a part of the neighbourhood in which the community lives, so these families – most of whom belonged to the Mocatta family – wanted to open a branch synagogue nearer their homes. Permission was refused under Ascama [Law] No. 1 which provided, under penalty of excommunication, that no other synagogue might be established within six miles of Bevis Marks.

At Bevis Marks there had been pressure for reforms since the beginning of the century: complaints were that attendance was poor (because of the distance), conduct in the synagogue was deplorable, the religious education of the children was trivial, and most of the instruction, the synagogue announcements and such sermons as were delivered, were still given in Spanish and Portuguese. In addition, there was no choir.

The problems in the Ashkenazi synagogue in Duke's Place were much the same: the Hebrew of the services was said to be gabbled, and the practice of making money offerings during the services was described as an abuse. The Sephardi and Ashkenazi communities remained aloof and hardly intermarried.

The aims of the West London Synagogue of British Jews were to establish a local place of worship to which the Jews in this country, irrespective of origin, might belong; where a revised form of service would be performed, at hours more suitable to the habits of the day; and where the children might have religious instruction from competent teachers.

A new prayer book would be used, containing the best of the Sephardi and Ashkenazi versions, with additions from old liturgies and poets; and the Sephardi pronunciation – being the more accurate – would be employed.

Daniel Mocatta, President of the Elders at Bevis Marks, became the first president of the congregation.

The first West London Synagogue of British Jews was in Burton Street, near the present Euston Station, and was consecrated on 27 January 1842. A week before that, however, the congregation had been excommunicated by both the Ashkenazi and Sephardi authorities.

The reformers were not permitted burial in a Jewish cemetery until, two years later, they acquired their own in Balls Pond Road, Islington.

They could not celebrate marriages in their synagogue under the new Acts of Parliament because Sir Moses Montefiore, then President of the Board of Deputies, refused 'to consider the place of worship in Burton Street to be a synagogue', although his brother Horatio was one of the founders. And when a Bill was introduced into Parliament to enable Jews to be married there, Sir Moses tried to persuade the Prime Minister, Lord Palmerston, against it.

But the congregation continued to grow and by 1849 it had to take a larger building at 50 Margaret Street, Cavendish Square, W1 (of which the plans are still to be seen in the library of the Royal Institute of British Architects).

In 1851 organ music began to be used on the Sabbath – an organ originally built in 1870 by the same firm who built the organ in London's Albert Hall is still in use today. Confirmation services were introduced for both girls and boys.

By 1870 the membership had increased again, to about 150 families (there are over 2,000 today), and a search began for a larger site for the synagogue. Eventually they succeeded in obtaining a lease from Lord Portman of premises near the Edgware Road.

Little has been changed in the design of the synagogue since it was erected in 1870, except for the reading desk which originally stood in the centre and was moved to the east side at the end of the last century. From its very beginning, however, the synagogue has had poor acoustics, and a remedy was only found in 1959 when amplifiers were installed.

The beautiful pattern on the ceiling was damaged during the Second World War and afterwards money was collected for its repainting. When the full effects of the Holocaust were seen and understood, however, the money was used instead to set up a home for child concentration camp survivors.

LIBERAL

Ealing Liberal Synagogue

Lynton Avenue, Drayton Green, W13   997 2580 and
567 5541

A small, friendly congregation with a reputation for its warm
welcome, says the synagogue's secretary. It has a number of
social activities – details on request. The synagogue building is a
small converted church, pine-clad and with small stained-glass
windows. The congregation has existed for over 40 years.
Certain Shabbat services are preceded by a Chavurah supper or
lunch.

West Central Liberal Synagogue

109 Whitfield Street, W1   636 7627

The key figures in the establishment of this congregation were
women – the sisters Lily and Marian Montagu, daughters of a
strictly Orthodox Jew, Samuel Montagu MP, a banker who later
became the first Lord Swaythling.

In 1893 Lily Montagu began to help run a Bible class in
Bloomsbury, and from this the two sisters developed the West
Central Jewish Girls' Club. All club meetings contained Liberal
prayers since Lily Montagu became aware that the traditional
form of Judaism had no appeal for many of the young people of
the day, who were therefore giving up their Jewish heritage.

She wrote an article for the *Jewish Quarterly Review* on this
subject, which aroused the interest of a number of prominent
Jews, and with their help the Jewish Religious Union was
formed in 1902. Services were held in an hotel in Marylebone,
and were the first services in this country to have many of the
prayers in English.

The Liberal Jewish Synagogue was established in 1911, and
in 1913 Lily Montagu started the West Central Section of the
Jewish Religious Union.

The West Central area of London was well populated with
Jews: a mainly Jewish market and Jewish shops and restaurants
abounded in the area.

The Section was hampered by two things: the first was lack of
money, for most of their members were far from prosperous,

and the second was that membership came mostly from the members and ex-members of the West Central Jewish Girls' Club, so they had few men. For these reasons they were not strong enough to form a congregation, nor could they afford to engage a minister.

The services were therefore conducted mainly by Lily Montagu until, in 1928, the Liberal Jewish Synagogue appointed Rabbi Solomon Starrels as their third minister, and he was permitted by them to serve as minister to the West Central Section.

The first service of the congregation took place on 8 September 1928, and from then on regular services were held which included choral and organ music, with prayers in Hebrew and English. Women members have always taken part in the services and served on the council and committees of the congregation.

In 1943 the Union of Liberal and Progressive Synagogues awarded Lily Montagu the title of Lay Minister. She was then officially able to carry on all the duties of a minister, including officiating at weddings and funerals. She was the first Jewish woman minister in Great Britain, and conducted services in a gown and hat, but without a talit.

She was awarded the Order of the British Empire (OBE) in 1937 for outstanding social work, and in 1955 was made a Commander of the British Empire (CBE) for her services to Jewish organizations. She was one of the first women in England to be a Justice of the Peace, and for many years served as a magistrate in the Borough of St Pancras.

Lily Montagu died in 1963 in her 90th year, and Marian died two years later, aged 96. In 1970 the congregation gave their lease and building to the Union of Liberal and Progressive Synagogues for their headquarters, on condition that they would have continued use of it for their services and other activities. The building was appropriately renamed The Montagu Centre.

Synagogue Directory

All the synagogues in and around London are listed by synagogue movement. Further details can be obtained from movements' head offices, addresses and phone numbers of which are given at the top of each section. If telephoning from outside the London area, dial 01 before the number.

UNITED SYNAGOGUE

Head Office: Woburn House, Upper Woburn Place, WC1   387 4300

Barking & Becontree: 200 Becontree Avenue, Dagenham, Essex

Barnet: Eversleigh Road, New Barnet, Herts

Bayswater & Maida Vale: Andover Road, Kilburn Park Road, NW6

Belmont: 101 Vernon Drive, Stanmore, Middx

Borehamwood & Elstree: Croxdale Road, Borehamwood, Herts

Bushey & District: 177–189 Sparrows Herne, Bushey Heath, Herts

Catford & Bromley: 6 Crantock Road, Catford, SE6

Central: Great Portland Street, W1

Chelsea: Smith Terrace, Smith Street, SW3

Chigwell & Hainault: Limes Avenue, Limes Farm, Chigwell, Essex

Cockfosters and North Southgate: Old Farm Avenue, N14

Cricklewood: 131 Walm Lane, NW2

Dollis Hill: Parkside, NW2

Ealing: 15 Grange Road, W5

East Ham & Manor Park: 28 Carlyle Road, E12

East London: 52 Rectory Square, Stepney Green, E1

Edgware: Edgware Way, Edgware, Middx

Edmonton & Tottenham: 41 Lansdowne Road, N17

Elm Park: 75 Woburn Avenue, Hornchurch, Essex

Enfield & Winchmore Hill: 53 Wellington Road, Enfield, Middx

Epsom: Prospect Place, Epsom, Surrey

Finchley: Kinloss Gardens, N3

Finsbury Park: Green Lanes, N4

Golders Green: 41 Dunstan Road, NW11

Hackney: Brenthouse Road, E9

Hammersmith & West Kensington: 71 Brook Green, W6

Hampstead: 1 Dennington Park Road, NW6

Hampstead Garden Suburb: Norrice Lea, Lyttleton Road, N2

Harold Hill: Trowbridge Road, Harold Hill, Essex

Hemel Hempstead: Morton House, Midland Road, Hemel Hempstead, Herts

Hendon: Raleigh Close, NW4

Highams Park & Chingford: Marlborough Road, E4

Highgate: Grimshaw Close, North Road, N6

High Wycombe: 33 Hampden Road, High Wycombe, Bucks

Hornsey & Wood Green: Wightman Road, N8

Hounslow: 98 Staines Road, Hounslow, Middx

Ilford: 24 Beehive Lane, Ilford, Essex

Kenton: Shaftesbury Avenue, Kenton, Middx

Kingsbury: Kingsbury Green, NW9

Kingston & Surbiton: 33–35 Uxbridge Road, Kingston, Surrey

Marble Arch: 32 Great Cumberland Place, W1

Mill Hill: Station Road, Mill Hill, NW7

Muswell Hill: 31 Tetherdown, N10

New: Egerton Road, N16

Newbury Park: 23 Wessex Close, Suffolk Road, Newbury Park, Essex

New West End: St Petersburgh Place, W2

Palmers Green & Southgate: Brownlow Road, N11

Pinner: 1 Cecil Park, Pinner, Middx

Potters Bar & Brookmans Park: Enquiries: 77-56166

Richmond: 8 Sheen Road, Richmond

Romford: 25 Eastern Road, Romford, Essex

Ruislip: Shenley Avenue, Ruislip Manor, Middx

St Albans: Oswald Road, St Albans, Herts

St John's Wood: 37–41 Grove End Road, NW8

South-East London: 200 New Cross Road, SE14

South Hampstead: Eton Road, NW3

South London: 55 Leigham Court Road, SW16

South Tottenham: Crowland Road, N15

South-West London: 104 Bolingbroke Grove, SW11

Staines: Westbrook Road, South Street, Staines

Stanmore & Canons Park: London Road, Stanmore, Middx

Sutton: 14 Cedar Road, Sutton, Surrey

Wanstead & Woodford: 20 Churchfields, South Woodford, E18

Watford: 16 Nascot Road, Watford, Herts

Welwyn Garden City: Handside Lane, Welwyn Garden City, Herts

Wembley: Forty Avenue, Wembley, Middx

West Ham & Upton Park: 93–95 Earlham Grove, E7

Willesden & Brondesbury: 143–145 Brondesbury Park, NW2

Woodside Park: Woodside Park Road, N12

FEDERATION OF SYNAGOGUES

Head Office: 9–11 Greatorex St, E1   247 4471

Ahavath Shalom (Neasden): Clifford Way, NW10

Bethnal Green Great (Tifereth Israel): 11–15 Bethnal Green Road, E1

Congregation of Jacob: 351–353 Commercial Road, Stepney, E1

Croydon & District: 30 Elmwood Road, Croydon, Surrey

East London Central: 38–40 Nelson Street, E1

Emet V'Shalom (Maida Vale Beth Hamedrash): 131 Elgin Avenue, W9

Fieldgate Street Great: 41 Fieldgate Street, E1

Finchley Central: Redbourne Avenue, N3

Great Garden Street: 7–9 Greatorex Street, E1

Greenford: 39–45 Oldfield Lane South, Greenford, Middx

Ilford Federation: 16 Coventry Road, Ilford, Essex

Leytonstone & Wanstead: 2 Fillebrook Road, E11

Machzike Hadath: 3 Highfield Road, NW11

Notting Hill: 206–208 Kensington Park Road, W11

Ohel Shem: 263 Chamberlayne Road, NW10

Sha'are Shomayim (Clapton): 47 Lea Bridge Road, E5

Shepherd's Bush, Fulham & District: 1a Poplar Grove, W6

Shomrei Hadath: 527a Finchley Road, NW3

Sinai: 54 Woodstock Avenue, NW11

Springfield: 202 Upper Clapton Road, E5

Stamford Hill Beth Hamedrash: 26 Lampard Grove, N16

Tottenham: 366 High Road, N17

West Hackney: 233a Amhurst Road, E8

Woolwich & District: Anglesea Road, Woolwich, SE8

Yavneh: 25 Ainsworth Road, E9

Yeshurun: Fernhurst Gardens, Edgware, Middx

UNION OF ORTHODOX HEBREW CONGREGATIONS

Head Office: 40 Queen Elizabeth's Walk, N16   802 6226 and 802 6227

Adath Yisroel: 40 Queen Elizabeth's Walk, N16

Adath Yisroel Tottenham Beth Hamedrash: 55 Ravensdale Road, N16

Beth Hamedrash Torah Etz Chayim: 69 Lordship Road, N16

Edgware Adath Yisroel: 261 Hale Lane, Edgware, Middx

Hampstead Adath Yisroel (Sarah Klausner Memorial Synagogue): 10a Cranfield Gardens, NW6

Hendon Adath Yisroel: 11 Brent Street, NW4

North Hendon Adath Yisroel: Holders Hill Road, NW4

INDEPENDENT SYNAGOGUES

Golders Green Beth Hamedrash Congregation: The Riding, Golders Green Road, NW11   455 2974

Lubavitch: 115 Stamford Hill, N16   800 0022

New London: 33 Abbey Road, St John's Wood, NW8 328 1026 and 328 1027

New North London: The Manor House, 80 East End Road, N3

Persian Hebrew Congregation: East Bank, Stamford Hill, N16 800 9261

Sandy's Row: 4a Sandy's Row, Middlesex Street, E1

West End Great: 21 Dean Street, W1   437 1873 and 437 1874

Western: Crawford Place, W1   723 9333 (Sec)

Westminster: Rutland Gardens, Knightsbridge, SW7   584 3953

SEPHARDI

Spanish & Portuguese Jews' Congregation
Head Office: 2 Ashworth Road, W9   289 2573

Bevis Marks: St Mary Axe, EC3

Lauderdale Road: Maida Vale, W9

Spanish & Portuguese: 8 St James's Gardens, W11

Wembley: 46 Forty Avenue, Wembley, Middx

Other Sephardi congregations in London include:

Aden Jews' Congregation: 117 Clapton Common, E5

Eastern Jewry: Station Hall, Newbury Park, Ilford, Essex

Holland Park: St James's Gardens, W11

Jacob Benjamin Elias Synagogue: 140 Stamford Hill, N16

Neveh Shalom Community: 352–354 Preston Road, Harrow, Middx

Ohel David Eastern: Broadwalk Lane, Golders Green, NW11

REFORM

Headquarters: The Manor House Centre for Judaism, 80 East End Road, N3   349 4731

Bromley & District: 28 Highland Road, Bromley, Kent

Buckhurst Hill: No premises. Enquiries: 508 8652

Edgware & District: 118 Stonegrove, Edgware, Middx

Finchley: Fallowcourt Avenue, N12

Hampstead: 56 Lymington Road, NW6

Hendon: Danescroft Avenue, NW4

Middlesex New: 39 Bessborough Road, Harrow, Middx

North-Western: Alyth Gardens, NW11

Radlett & Bushey: 118 Watling Street, Radlett, Herts

Settlement Synagogue: Beaumont Grove, E1

Southgate: 45 High Street, N14

South-West Essex: Oaks Lane, Newbury Park, Essex

Wembley: Enquiries: 907 5225

West London Synagogue of British Jews: 34 Upper Berkeley Street, W1

Wimbledon & District: 44–46 Worple Road, SW19

LIBERAL

Headquarters of Union of Liberal and Progressive Synagogues: 109 Whitfield Street, W1   580 1663

Barkingside Progressive: 129 Perryman's Farm Road, Barkingside, Ilford, Essex

Belsize Square: 51 Belsize Square, NW3

Chiltern Progressive: 289 Birdsfoot Lane, Luton, Beds

Ealing: Lynton Avenue, Drayton Green, W13

Finchley Progressive: 54a Hutton Grove, N12

Hertsmere Progressive: High Street, Elstree, Herts

Kingston: Rushett Road, Long Ditton, Surrey

Liberal Jewish: 28 St John's Wood Road, NW8

North London Progressive: 100 Amhurst Park, N16

Northwood & Pinner: Oaklands Gate, Northwood, Middx

Southgate: 75 Chase Road, N14

South London: 1 Prentis Road, SW16

The Settlement Synagogue: c/o Stepney Jewish Settlement, Beaumont Grove, E1

Wembley: 326 Preston Road, Harrow, Middx

West Central: 109 Whitfield Street, W1

Woodford & District: Marlborough Road, George Lane, E18

Mikvaot (Ritual Baths)

Central Mikvaot Board
40 Queen Elizabeth's Walk, N16   802 6226

Ilford Mikvah
463 Cranbrook Road, Ilford, Essex   554 5450

Lordship Park Mikvah
55 Lordship Park, N16   800 9621

North-West London Communal Mikvah
10a Shirehall Lane, NW4   202 7692

North London Mikvah
Adjoining 40 Queen Elizabeth's Walk, N16   802 2554

Satmar Mikvah
62 Filey Avenue, N16   806 3961

Stamford Hill Mikvah
26 Lampard Grove, N16   806 3880

United Synagogue Mikvah
Kingsbury Green, NW9   205 3038 (day) 204 6390 (evening)

Meeting People

Whatever your age or interests, it is not difficult to find a group of like-minded people in London with whom to share them.

Synagogues often have a range of social activities, from youth clubs to friendship clubs for the over 60s, from bridge evenings to dinner dances. Many events are advertized in the *Jewish Chronicle* or other publications.

There are also associations and clubs dealing with specific interests, such as golf and country clubs for the sporty; orchestras and dramatic societies for those who like to watch, listen or take part in concerts and productions; cultural societies that hold lectures, outings and other events.

If you have a particular hobby or interest not covered on these pages, get in touch with the Central Enquiry Desk and Communal Diary (which is under the auspices of the Board of Deputies). They will help you find a suitable group, if one exists. Their number is 387 4044 (dial 01 first if telephoning from outside London).

Youth Clubs

The following youth clubs have their own premises and youth leaders. You can phone them for information during office hours. They generally have meetings on different nights for different age groups, so check which are appropriate.

Remember, though, that no youth clubs will be open on Shabbat, and none have residential facilities.

They are all affiliated to AJY (see page 122).

Barkingside Jewish Youth Centre
Carlton Drive, Barkingside, Ilford, Essex   551 1596

Brady Maccabi Youth & Community Centre
4 Manor Park Crescent, Edgware, Middx   952 2948

Kenton Jewish Youth Centre
Shaftesbury Avenue, Kenton   907 8054

Kinnor Jewish Youth & Community Centre
366a Stag Lane, NW9   204 6211

Maccabi Association London
Maccabi House, 73 Compayne Gardens, NW6   328 4776

Oxford & St Georges North London Jewish Centre
120 Oakleigh Road North, N20   446 3101/2

Redbridge Jewish Youth & Community Centre
Sinclair House, Woodford Bridge Road, Redbridge, Ilford,
Essex   551 0017

SPEC Jewish Youth & Community Centre
Alderman House, 87 Brookside South, East Barnet, Herts
368 5117

Victoria Community Centre
Egerton Road, N16   802 1141

Western Jewish Youth Centre
39 Brendon Street, W1   258 0179

Students and Singles

If you're new to London and would like to meet other young
people, there are a number of ways of finding out what's going
on in your area.

Many synagogues have clubs which you could visit, or you could go along to a youth centre which has its own premises and qualified youth leaders (see page 120).

If you're a student, make your way straight to:

Hillel House
1–2 Endsleigh Street, WC1

For everything from advice on accommodation to social events. This is also the home of the Union of Jewish Students, the Israel Students Association, B'nai B'rith, and a number of other important groups.

If you are not a student try:

The Western Centre
39 Brendon Street, W1

This is a non-commercial singles' meeting place. Here you'll also find a women's group, coffee shop and other activities.

Or you could simply look in the *Jewish Chronicle*, forthcoming events section, for details of parties, discos, quiz evenings and other social activities (see page 132).

The *Jewish Chronicle* also carries regular advertizements for meetings of the Jewish Gay Group. Addresses for this and the Jewish Feminist Group appear under 'Miscellaneous Organizations' (see pages 175–178).

Here is a selection of organizations which you might find helpful.

The Association for Jewish Youth (AJY)
50 Lindley Street, E1   790 6407

This is the central organization for Jewish youth, and to which nearly all of the youth organizations are affiliated.

They will always be happy to give you information about youth groups, meeting places and social events in London. They cannot, however, help you with accommodation.

AJY provides a number of services for youth organizations, including an advisory service, a library for youth workers, a

When they told me B.B. was at Hillel House
I naturally assumed it was Brigitte Bardot.
It turned out to be the B'nai B'rith.

residential centre for youth groups and a number of training courses. It also organizes inter-club sports events.

Association of Jewish Sixth Formers (AJ6)
1–2 Endsleigh Street, WC1   388 3776

This deals with sixth-form groups and assemblies and prepares students for university life.

Betar
71 Compayne Gardens, NW6   624 0976

A Zionist youth movement, with groups in London – Golders Green, Hendon, etc – and other branches in Birmingham, Leeds and Manchester.

B'nai B'rith Youth Organization
1–2 Endsleigh Street, WC1   387 3115

BBYO has programmes for 13–16 year-olds, young adults (18–25), and students – Hillel House provides a Jewish address on campus for thousands of Jewish students away from home.

It has groups throughout London, including Ilford, Ealing, Cockfosters and South London.

B'nei Akiva of Great Britain and Ireland
143 Brondesbury Park, NW2   459 2923

A religious Zionist youth movement with branches throughout the country. It has centres in major Jewish areas of London including Hendon, Kenton, St John's Wood and Willesden. Visitors are welcome at centres and at regular meetings on a variety of religious subjects. Age group 7 to school-leaving (17–18).

Ezra
2a Alba Gardens, NW11   458 5372

A religious youth movement with branches in London and Manchester. It is associated with Poale Agudat Israel.

Federation of Zionist Youth
523 Finchley Road, NW3   794 1987

FZY has a number of groups, primarily in North-West London and around Ilford and Chigwell. It is affiliated to the Zionist Federation of Great Britain and caters for age groups 16–18, 18–21, and 21+. Branches also in Glasgow, Leeds and Manchester.

Habonim-Dror
523 Finchley Road, NW3   435 9033

Habonim was formally launched in East London in 1928 by Wellesley Aron and described as a 'Jewish Cultural Youth Movement'; Dror began in Poland in the 1920s and was established in England in the 1950s.

The two movements merged in 1980 and this Zionist youth movement has groups throughout London – Chigwell, Elstree, Southgate, etc – as well as in most provincial cities.

Hanoar Hatzioni
31 Tetherdown, Muswell Hill, N10   444 7414

This is a Zionist youth movement with branches all over London, in areas such as Northwood, Muswell Hill and St John's Wood, as well as further afield in areas like Watford and Welwyn Garden City. It also has branches in provincial cities.

Jewish Guide Advisory Council
c/o 48 Stonegrove, Edgware, Middx   958 5931

Co-ordinates Jewish Brownie Packs and Guide Companies. There are over 30 of these throughout London.

Jewish Lads' and Girls' Brigade
Camperdown, 3 Beechcroft Road, E18   989 8990

There are Brigade companies throughout the UK.

Jewish Scout Advisory Council
c/o 313 Preston Road, Kenton, Middx   940 6562

Co-ordinates Jewish Cub and Scout Packs, with companies throughout London, in areas such as Bushey, Golders Green, Pinner and Southgate.

Jewish Youth Study Groups
Woburn House, Upper Woburn Place, WC1   387 2681

A religious youth movement with groups in areas such as Ilford, Kingston, Luton and Middlesex, as well as in provincial cities.

Jewish Youth Voluntary Service
AJY House, 50 Lindley Street, E1   790 6407

Part of AJY (see page 122), JYVS is an independent organization with a full-time director and a large number of individuals (aged 13–25) making up a volunteer force which gives practical assistance to a number of causes.

The variety of projects covered includes looking after children, helping old-age pensioners, the mentally and physically handicapped, running hospital radio stations, a toy library, plus cleaning, gardening, decorating.

Lubavitch Foundation
107 Stamford Hill, N16   800 0022

Has a range of religious youth groups.

Maccabi Union
'Annandale', North End Road, NW11   458 9488

This services the network of Maccabi clubs in the UK, which offer amateur sports, cultural and non-political communal activities, such as drama, judo, bridge, etc.

Reform Synagogue Youth-Netzer
The Sternberg Centre for Judaism, 80 East End Road, N3
349 4731

A youth movement which also services Reform Synagogue youth groups nationally. There are over a dozen groups at synagogues in and around London.

Satmah
(Students at the Manor House)
80 East End Road, N3   346 2288

Arranges vacation-time seminars, Friday night celebrations and a student counselling service.

ULPSNYC
(Union of Liberal and Progressive Synagogues Network of Youth Clubs)
109 Whitfield Street, W1   580 1663

A youth movement which services Reform Synagogue Youth Groups nationally. It organizes quizzes, mini-weekends, study seminars, festival celebrations and leadership tours to Israel.

United Synagogue Youth and Community Services Department
c/o Hendon Community Centre, 18 Raleigh Close, NW4
202 7529

This services the youth and community work of the United Synagogue and has activities as far afield as Stanmore, Mill Hill and Sutton.

The Unity Group
Stanmore Cottage, Old Church Lane, Stanmore, Middx
954 0257

Has groups for young mentally handicapped Jewish children as well as integration schemes in many Jewish youth centres.

WUPJYS
(World Union for Progressive Judaism – Youth Section)
109 Whitfield Street, W1   580 1663

This group produces a newsletter with details of Chavurah – Friday-night meals and meetings, shiurim (study groups), parties, visits to groups in other countries, etc.

Social Groups and Cultural Societies

See also Miscellaneous Organizations (pages 175–8); Music, Dance and Drama (pages 149–54); and Adult Education (pages 135–7).

Association of Jewish Friendship Clubs
Woburn House, Upper Woburn Place, WC1   387 8980

Under the auspices of the League of Jewish Women and the United Synagogue, has groups in synagogues throughout London for the over-60s. Ask at your local synagogue or contact the address above for a list of clubs.

B'nai B'rith
B'nai B'rith, Hillel House, 1–2 Endsleigh Street, WC1
387 5278 and 387 5954

Has adult Jewish education programmes covering local and national schemes – from lodge study groups and one-day seminars to national weekend seminars which cover a particular theme in Jewish history, life or culture.

JACS
Describes itself as a 'cultural society for the active retired'. Fifteen branches – from Northwood to Ilford, with 3,000 members, meet once a week on Wednesdays or Thursdays on synagogue premises. Activities include visits to museums, outings to the theatre and cinema, etc.

Your local synagogue will tell you if it has a JACS club and whether membership of it is still open. Or contact Mrs A. Pearlman on 958 8867.

The Jewish Historical Society of England
33 Seymour Place, W1

This society was founded in 1893 to promote the study of the history of the Jews of the British Empire. From October to June or July it holds monthly meetings at which papers and popular presentations are delivered on various aspects of Anglo-Jewish history.

Membership of the society entitles you to a range of facilities, including free publications and use of the Mocatta Library (see page 144).

Jewish Senior Ramblers
This is one of the many rambling clubs in London and offers senior citizens the chance to take in some country air while walking through the Home Counties of Kent, Surrey, etc. Details from Irene Gunston, 229 8373.

League of Jewish Women
Woburn House, Upper Woburn Place, WC1   387 7688

Founded in 1943, this is a non-political Jewish women's voluntary service organization. Members carry out a wide range of services including helping in hospitals, delivering meals on wheels to the housebound, and providing day-care for elderly and/or disabled people.

The organization also offers, through conferences, seminars and conventions, the chance to meet other Jewish women.

The Sternberg Centre
The Manor House, 80 East End Road, N3   346 2288

This is a broadly-based intellectual, cultural and educational centre with a wide range of activities including lectures and exhibitions.

It is the home of the Manor House Society, a cultural and intellectual society; the Museum of the East End (see page 146); Leo Baeck College, the seminary that trains non-Orthodox rabbis; a book and Judaica service (see page 79); the facilities of the Leo Baeck College Library (see page 143); a coffee shop and cafeteria.

Younger JNF for Great Britain and Ireland
Harold Poster House, Kingsbury Circle, NW9   204 9911

Offers fund-raising and social activities for groups all over the country. Age 18–27.

Zionist Federation of Great Britain and Ireland
741 High Street, Finchley, N12   446 1477

About a dozen groups meet in different parts of London and have monthly meetings with a speaker.

Golf and Country Clubs

The following are open to Jewish membership.

Abridge Golf and Country Club
Stapleford Tawney, Essex   040-28396

Coombe Hill Golf Club
Golf Club Drive, Kingston Hill, Surrey   942 2284

Members only. Guests can play as long as they have a handicap. There is a club-house, TV room.

Dyrham Park Country Club
Galley Lane, Barnet, Herts   440 3361

Open to members and guests. Tennis courts and a swimming pool; also holds functions.

Hartsbourne Country Club
Hartsbourne Avenue, Bushey Heath, Herts   950 1133

Visitors must be signed in by a member. Has a golf course, swimming pool from May–September, snooker and card room, sauna, TV room. To become a member you have to be proposed and seconded by full members.

Kendal Hall Country Club
Watling Street, Radlett, Herts   779 5911

Visitors must be signed in by a member. Tennis courts, an open-air swimming pool, squash court, restaurant.

Potters Bar Golf Club
Darkes Lane, Potters Bar, Herts   0707 52020

Open to visitors. Has a golf course, club-house, professional shop where you can get lessons and have equipment repaired, showers, restaurant, bar, and large car park.

Bridge Clubs

Acol Bridge Club
86 West End Lane, NW6   624 7407

Bridge Builders
Michael Sobell House, Limes Avenue, NW11   458 7411

Harold Shogger's 77 Bridge Club
81a Brent Street, NW4   202 4718

Many synagogues have Bridge Clubs, and social committees often hold Bridge evenings. You'll often find these advertised in the 'Club and Charitable Activities' section of the *Jewish Chronicle*.

The Media

Newspapers and Magazines

The earliest Jewish newspaper in the English language was the London *Hebrew Intelligencer* (1823), which lasted for just three issues. It was succeeded by the *Voice of Jacob* (1841–1848) and the *Jewish Chronicle* (founded in 1841). The following publications are available today.

Jewish Chronicle
25 Furnival Street, EC4   405 9252

This is the oldest extant Jewish periodical, founded in 1841. It reaches the majority of Jewish homes in the country, with its highest readership in London.

It is published every Friday and contains everything from Middle East news to local fund-raising efforts; it also has a special 'London Extra' section dealing with events in the capital, a quarterly free colour magazine, and regular supplements on a number of subjects from business to interior design.

Classified sections cover everything from articles for sale to job vacancies, from social events to births and barmitzvahs. You'll also find advertizements from estate agents, catering firms, marriage bureaux, etc.

The '*JC*' is available from major newsagents (eg W. H. Smith) in areas such as Golders Green, Ilford, Edgware, etc. It is also on sale in a number of venues in Central London, which include underground station kiosks at Tottenham Court Road, Piccadilly Circus, Oxford Circus, Green Park, Knightsbridge and Queensway; in kiosks and newsagents in Great Portland Street, Old Compton Street, Marylebone High Street, Baker Street; and outside the Cumberland Hotel and the Mount Royal Hotel.

If you are unable to obtain a copy, you can get in touch with the *Jewish Chronicle* at the above address, who keep spare copies.

'. . . *and now four questions from a listener in Stamford Hill which begin "Mah nishtana ha-leila ha-zeh . . ."* '

Jewish Tribune
97 Stamford Hill, N16   800 6688

An Orthodox newspaper published every Thursday, it carries general news and advertizing. Both sides of its last page are in Yiddish. It is distributed to shops in areas with a large Jewish population.

Jewish Quarterly
P.O. Box 488, London, NW3   431 2225

This magazine was established in 1953 and is published four times a year by the Jewish Literary Trust Ltd. It carries articles, poems, opinions on subjects from art to politics, advertisements, etc, and is available at newsagents in Jewish areas, including branches of W. H. Smith and Lavells.

Jewish Review
26 Golders Green Road, NW11   455 2243

The 'voice of Religious Zionism', this journal is published three or four times a year by the Mizrachi-Hapoel Hamizrachi Federation of Great Britain and Ireland. It has features, book reviews, carries a small number of advertisements, and is available by subscription.

Manna
The Manor House Society, 80 East End Road, N3   346 2288

This is a quarterly journal published by the Manor House Society, launched in 1984 as a national Jewish cultural and intellectual society 'devoted to the promotion of excellence in the arts'. It has book reviews, provocative articles by well-known writers, etc. Details from the address above.

Broadcasting

You Don't Have to be Jewish
Radio London (MW 206m, VHF/FM 94.9)   Sun 9.32 am
Thurs 6.33 pm

A twice-weekly magazine programme produced in conjunction with the Board of Deputies and presented by Michael Freedland. It features phone-ins, interviews with people in Israel, book reviews, debates in the studio (often featuring rabbis), music, chats with famous personalities, etc.

Adult Education

Hebrew and Yiddish Lessons

If you'd like to learn Hebrew or Yiddish, or brush up your existing knowledge, a number of day and evening classes are held throughout London.

Many synagogues run adult Hebrew classes and a few have Yiddish Circles; the *Jewish Chronicle* also carries regular advertisements for courses in these languages.

MODERN HEBREW CLASSES

These are available at a number of adult education centres (see list on page 136), as well as through the following organizations:

Hampstead Garden Suburb Institute
Central Square, NW11   455 9951

Hillel House
1–2 Endsleigh Street, WC1   387 3115

Maccabi Ulpan
71 Compayne Gardens, NW6   455 2288

Wizo
105–107 Gloucester Place, W1   486 2691

Yakar
2 Egerton Gardens, NW4   202 5551 and 202 5552

YIDDISH LESSONS

These are available at a number of adult education centres (see list below), as well as at:

Yakar
Address as previous page.

ADULT EDUCATION CENTRES

The following centres currently offer classes in modern Hebrew or Yiddish. Telephone numbers only are given since each centre has a variety of different venues.

Bear in mind that you'll have to sign up for at least a term, and that not all classes are for beginners.

HEBREW

Central Institute of Adult Education
388 7106

Chelsea-Westminster Adult Education Institute
589 2044

The City Lit
242 9872   (Language department: 430 0545)

Hackney Adult Education Institute
533 2426

Hammersmith and North Kensington Adult Education Centre
969 0303

Hampstead Garden Suburb Institute
455 9951

Marylebone-Paddington Adult Education Institute
286 1900   722 5151

Polytechnic of Central London
580 2020   (Language department: 486 5811)

Thamesside Adult Education Institute
855 9044

YIDDISH

The City Lit
242 9872   (Language department: 430 0545)

Hackney Adult Education Institute
533 2426

South Lewisham Adult Education Institute
698 4113   (NB This is for informal chatting and at present
there is no tutor)

Further information about adult eductation centres can be
obtained from *Floodlight*, the Inner London Education Authority's guide to part-time day and evening classes in Inner London. It is published before the autumn term begins each year
and you can buy it from stationers and bookshops, including
W. H. Smith, for around 50p. Alternatively, ring the ILEA
Information Centre at County Hall on 633 1066.

For individual tuition in your own home you could also
consider a language school such as Foreign Language Services
(263 3996).

Jewish Studies

Many synagogues have adult education classes and lectures
where you can learn everything from how to follow a service to
how to conduct one. Your local synagogue should be able to
advise on suitable courses. (See also Synagogues section.)

The following centres also offer courses for those interested in learning about the history or philosophy of Judaism.

The City Lit
242 9872   (various venues)

Has courses in Jewish history and literature.

Hampstead Garden Suburb Institute
Central Square, NW11   455 9951

Among its courses of Jewish interest is one called 'The Jew in the Modern World', which is presented in association with the Spiro Institute (see below).

The Spiro Institute
3 St John's Wood Road, NW8   286 6701

Offers courses in Jewish history and culture, has a film club, a drama workshop, and organizes music evenings, lectures and recitals. Forthcoming events are advertized in the *Jewish Chronicle*.

Yakar
2 Egerton Gardens, NW4   202 5551

Offers everything from beginners' courses in Judaism (how to read and understand the text of the prayer-book, insights into the weekly synagogue reading, etc) to more advanced study (courses designed to show how Talmudic discussion works, in-depth study of the Bible, how different Jewish thinkers have understood some of the basic concepts of Judaism, etc). Also a series of regular shiurim for those with a strong background in Jewish learning.

Sightseeing

Art Galleries

The following galleries would be of particular interest to Jewish visitors. Bear in mind that many are closed on bank holidays, and some charge an entrance fee. If you are telephoning from outside the London area, dial 01 before the number.

Ben Uri Art Society
21 Dean Street, W1   437 2852
Mon–Thurs 10 am–5 pm

Large gallery exhibiting works by Jewish artists, both contemporary and past; also holds exhibitions and sells paintings. Holds lectures and music recitals. Details of forthcoming events are displayed in the gallery.

Marlborough Fine Art
6 Albemarle Street, W1   629 5161
Mon–Fri 10 am–5.30 pm   Sat 10 am–12.30 pm

Holds one-man exhibitions upstairs, but works by Jewish artists downstairs include paintings by R. B. Kitaj, Avigdor Arikha, Mordecai Ardon, Frank Auerbach, Oskar Kokoschka and Kurt Schwitters.

National Gallery
Trafalgar Square, WC2   839 3321
Mon–Sat 10 am–6 pm   Sun 2 pm–6 pm

Has a massive collection of world-famous paintings of different periods and schools. Those of Jewish interest include paintings by Camille Pissarro (1830–1903): 'View from Louveciennes' (circa 1870); 'The Boulevard Montmartre at Night', painted in 1897 from a room in an hotel; 'The Côte des Boeufs at L'Hermitage, near Pontoise', 1877; 'The Louvre Under Snow', 1902; and 'Lower Norwood Under Snow', painted on the first of Pissarro's several visits to England. Also 'An Old Man Writing' by Jozef Israels, known as 'The Philosopher' in Israels' lifetime (1824–1911); and 'Fishermen Carrying a Drowned Man', said to have been painted by Israels in 1861.

National Portrait Gallery
2 St Martin's Place, W2   930 1552
Mon–Fri 10 am–5 pm   Sat 10 am–6 pm   Sun 2 pm–6 pm

Enormous selection of both Jewish 'sitters' and portraits by Jewish artists. Subjects include: members of the Rothschild and Montefiore families; Disraeli and his father, Isaac D'Israeli; violinist Yehudi Menuhin; Leonard Woolf (husband of authoress Virginia Woolf). Self-portraits by Jacob Epstein (in bronze), Mark Gertler, Jacob Kramer, Solomon J. Solomon, war artist and poet Isaac Rosenberg. Also paintings by Sir William Rothenstein, Emanuel Levy, Mervyn Levy, Jacob Kramer, Gertler, Enoch Seeman, Isaac Seeman, Solomon J. Solomon, Moritz Oppenheim, etc. Not all, however, are permanently on display.

Tate Gallery
Millbank, SW1   821 1313
Mon–Sat 10 am–6 pm   Sun 2 pm–6 pm

Large selection of works by Jewish artists, including Israeli artists Mordecai Ardon, Moshe Castel and Sorel Etrog; Polish artist Jankel Adler; Chagall and Mark Gertler. Also many Jewish scenes, including 'Jews at Prayer' by Jacob Kramer (circa 1919), 'Jews Mourning in a Synagogue' by Sir William Rothenstein (1906), 'Jew and Gentile' by Arthur Boyd Houghton (1864), 'Orthodox Boys' by Bernard Perlin (1948), 'Interior of a Synagogue at the Time of Reading the Law' by Solomon Hart (1830). The collection rotates so that *all* the paintings mentioned may not necessarily be on show when you visit.

*Bearskin shmearskin. I still think
it looks like my booba's sheitel.*

Whitechapel Art Gallery

80 Whitechapel High Street, E1   377 0107
Tues–Sun 11 am–5 pm (except Wed 11 am–8 pm)

This gallery has a long association with the Jewish community
and often features works by local Jewish artists. There is no
permanent display, and the gallery is closed between exhibitions. It has an annual open exhibition which is limited to artists
who live in the East End (there are still many Jewish artists in
the area) – this takes place around January–February. The
Community Education Department also organizes one-man
exhibitions which are shown in and around Whitechapel.

In August 1986 the gallery is holding an exhibition of the
sights and sounds of the Jewish East End, in conjunction with
the Springboard Educational Trust.

Libraries

Arts Council Poetry Library

105 Piccadilly, W1   629 9495
Mon–Tues 10 am–5.30 pm   Wed–Fri 10 am–6 pm

Twentieth-century poetry library where you will find the work
of Isaac Rosenberg and other Jewish poets among the
anthologies.

British Library

Store Street, WC1   636 1544
Mon–Fri 9.30 am–4.45 pm   Sat 9.30 am–1 pm

The Oriental Section has one of the finest collections of Hebrew
books and manuscripts in the world – around 60,000 books and
3,000 manuscripts. They are available mainly for research –
visitors need to get a ticket at the Library Ticket Office or from
the British Museum in Great Russell Street, WC2.

Central Library

Bancroft Road, E1   980 4366
Mon–Fri 9 am–8 pm (Wed to 5 pm only)   Sat 9 am–5 pm

Specializes in information on the Jewish East End, and has a selection of pamphlets and books.

Guildhall Library & Art Gallery

Aldermanbury, EC2   606 3030
Mon–Sat 9.30 am–5 pm

In the London Collection are details of Jewish historical interest. There is also a Print and Photographs collection which has a number of exhibits of Jewish interest (this collection is only open Monday–Friday).

Hendon Public Library

The Burroughs, NW4   202 5625

This public library has a large selection of books of Jewish interest, from Jewish art to the Jewish Encyclopaedia, novels, statistical data, etc.

Institute of Contemporary History & Weiner Library Ltd

4 Devonshire Street, W1   636 7247
Mon–Fri 10 am–5.30 pm

A specialist collection of Germany 1933–1945, dealing with antisemitism and the Holocaust, and post-War German–Jewish relations. This library was founded by Alfred Weiner and concentrates mainly on antisemitism and racism.

Leo Baeck College Library

The Manor House Centre for Judaism, 80 East End Road, N3 349 4525
Mon–Thurs 10 am–4.30 pm   Fri 10 am–1 pm

This is a general library and visitors must make an appointment to visit it for the first time.

Lubavitch Lending Library
Lubavitch Foundation, 107–115 Stamford Hill, N16
800 0022
Mon–Thurs 10 am–4 pm   Fri 10 am–1 pm
Sun 10 am–12 noon   4 pm–8 pm

Has books on all Jewish subjects including about 2,500 English books dealing with Chasidic thought and philosophy, basic introductions to Judaism, traditional points of view, history, a woman's role in Judaism, dietary and marital laws, abortion, autopsy, as well as children's books, biographies, and approximately 8,000 Hebrew and Yiddish books on the Talmud and the Bible.

Mocatta Library (Incorporating the Library of the Jewish Historical Society of England)
University College London, Gower Street, WC1
387 7050 (extension 778)
Mon, Wed 2 pm–4 pm

This library of Jewish history and English Judaica, originally founded by philanthropist and bibliophile Frederic David Mocatta and presented to University College by the Jewish Historical Society of England in 1905, was destroyed in a German air-raid in 1940 and was reopened in 1954. It now includes the Hebraica and Judaica section of the Guildhall Library as well as a number of other important collections.

Stamford Hill Public Library
Portland Avenue, N16   985 8262
Mon, Tues, Thurs 9 am–8 pm   Wed, Sat 9 am–5 pm
Fri 9 am–6 pm

Has a large stock of books of Jewish interest.

Yakar Library
2 Egerton Gardens, NW4   202 5551 and 202 5552
Evenings from 7.30 pm   Sun morning

Jewish lending library with a reading room, wide range of books on Jewish history, philosophy, Israel, etc, plus resources for programming, offprints from journals, exhibitions.

Museums

The British Museum
Great Russell Street, WC1   636 1555
Mon–Sat 10 am–5 pm   Sun 2.30 pm–6 pm

The Department of Western Asiatic Antiquities holds material from ancient Palestine, from early times until the Byzantine period, including ancient Hebrew inscriptions, seals, pottery, weapons, etc. Also material from other areas which bears on ancient Israel and Judea. The Ancient Palestine Room (Room 24) contains the main range of material. It is situated on the ground floor and includes letters, pottery, ivories, etc.

Imperial War Museum
Lambeth Road, SE1   735 8922
Museum: *Mon–Sat 10 am–5.50 pm   Sun 2 pm–5.50 pm*
Reference Departments *(open by appointment)*: *Mon–Fri 10 am–5 pm*
Library: *Mon–Fri 10 am–5 pm*

Features a Second World War section, part of which is called 'Refugees' and deals with the concentration camps. Exhibits include documents, a pair of trousers, gas canisters, etc. Also a drawing by Felix Topolski.

There are also a number of reference departments which would be of interest:

The Department of Sound Records has recordings of interviews with refugees about their lives in Germany, experiences, and escape. It is open by appointment and you can listen to tapes and buy copies. A new project is currently being compiled of interviews with concentration camp survivors.

The Department of Documents has letters and diaries about Germany including Isaac Rosenberg sketches, manuscripts, and a few of his letters and personal papers.

The Art Department has three drawings by David Bomberg – one First World War drawing and two Second World War ones – as well as a selection of other works by Jewish artists, including a pastel by Gerhardt Frankl of a concentration camp victim.

The Photo Library has a number of photographs of concentration camp survivors and scenes – not recommended for young children. There is also a Reference Library.

Jewish Museum
Woburn House, Upper Woburn Place, WC1   388 4525
Tues–Thurs (and Fri from Apr–Sept) 10 am–4 pm   Sun (and Fri from Oct–Mar) 10 am–12.45 pm

Contains a collection of Jewish ceremonial art and objects relating to the Jewish community in Britain. There is also a collection of metalware, illuminated documents, portraits, prints and drawings, and other artefacts.

Madame Tussaud's
Marylebone Road, NW1   935 6861
Mon–Sun 10 am–5.30 pm

Has ever-changing selection of lifelike waxworks models, so look out for famous Jewish statesmen and well-known figures. Currently on display are British Prime Minister Benjamin Disraeli (1804–81, modelled in 1973) and David Ben-Gurion (1886–1973, modelled in 1970), Israel's first Prime Minister. Ben-Gurion is seen standing next to Anwar Sadat. It is perhaps fitting that the first model you meet at the entrance to the Chamber of Horrors is Adolf Hitler . . .

The Museum of the Jewish East End & Research Centre
80 East End Road, N3   346 2288
Sun–Thurs 10 am–5 pm

This museum was founded in 1983 with the objective of rescuing and preserving the heritage of the Jewish East End. On display is a series of walk-in tableaux and photographs representing all aspects of Jewish East End life – at work, at home, in

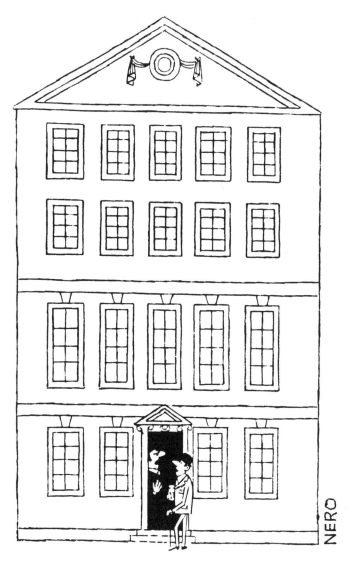

'*Is this house Jewish?*'
'*No. It's Georgian*'

the synagogue, at school and in leisure pursuits. Tableaux include an immigrant's home, a tailoring workshop, a display of baking and a 'workers' circle' (friendly society) scene. The many photographs, documents and objects reflect the everyday experiences of the mass of Jewish people who lived and worked in the East End earlier this century. The museum also has a range of activities which include a 'Family History Workshop' for those wishing to trace their roots, and an East End Research Group which is open to anyone with an active interest in the East End or Jewish social history.

National Army Museum
Royal Hospital Road, SW3   730 0717
Mon–Sat 10 am–5.30 pm   Sun 2 pm–5.30 pm

In the Flanders To The Falklands gallery is an officer's SD forage cap badge of the 38th, 40th and 42nd Battalions Royal Fusiliers (City of London Regiment), circa 1914. These battalions were recruited from Jewish volunteers.

Public Record Office
Chancery Lane, WC2   405 0741

The Public Record Office Museum was reopened for the Domesday Exhibition in April 1986. There are many records of Jewish interest in the Office, including a petition dated 24 March 1655 from Menasseh Ben Israel and six other London Jews asking Oliver Cromwell for permission to conduct religious services in their private homes.

The building which now houses the Museum is built on the site of the Rolls chapel, originally named the *Domus Conversorum* in the 13th century, and intended for converted Jews.

Royal Air Force Museum
Aerodrome Road, Hendon, NW9   205 2266
Mon–Sat 10 am–6 pm   Sun 2 pm–6 pm

On permanent display in the Battle of Britain Museum is a painting called 'Premonition', painted in 1937 and picturing London in the Blitz – three years ahead of the event! It is by

Jewish painter Walter Nessler, who left his native Germany before the War and after being interned served in the British Air Force throughout the War. The painting was presented to the museum in 1979, a year after it opened.

In the Bomber Command Museum is an avant garde painting by Jewish artist Alfred Hubermann, who did a complete tour of operations as an air gunner. The painting is called 'Impressions of Flying Over Germany'.

Incidentally, it is said that Hendon saw the first casualty of the Second World War. War was declared at 11 am on Sunday, 3 September 1939 and at 11.20 am a plane from Hendon crashed on take-off, killing the Jewish pilot. There is a memorial to him in a nearby cemetery.

Victoria and Albert Museum
Cromwell Road, SW7   589 6371
Mon–Thurs and Sat 11 am–5.50 pm   Sun 2.30 pm–5.50 pm

This museum has many exhibits of Jewish interest, including 19th-century textiles, manuscripts, metalwork and ceramics. Specific examples are Torah mantles, Chanucah lamps, a Dutch Esther scroll, a North-African wedding dress, wedding rings and spice candles.

Music, Dance and Drama

There are a number of choirs, orchestras, theatre groups and organizations that specialize in performing or promoting Jewish or Israeli music, dance and dramatic works. The following selection should give you some idea of the variety of activities available.

Ben Uri Orchestra
c/o Marylebone Evening Institute, Gateway School, NW1
723 1331 (after 6 pm)

The Matza soprano

An amateur symphony orchestra with a friendly, informal atmosphere that would welcome visiting musicians. It rehearses on Thursday nights.

British Israel Arts Foundation
126–134 Baker Street, W1   486 3867

This arts foundation publishes a quarterly programme of events, organizes concerts, tours, theatrical performances and exhibitions promoting the best of Israeli culture and art.

B'nai B'rith Music Festival
B'nai B'rith, Hillel House, 1–2 Endsleigh Street, WC1
387 5278 and 387 5954

This is a biennial event, the 1986 festival taking place from 15 June to 17 July as part of the 60th anniversary celebrations of B'nai B'rith in District 15 (Great Britain and Ireland).

The month-long festival of music of Jewish interest and significance takes place in major concert halls and special venues in London and elsewhere, and features music ranging from ancient prayer chants through vocal, choral, instrumental and orchestral music, opera and oratorio. There are synagogue services in diverse tradition – Orthodox, Reform and Liberal – featuring local choirs, as well as folk music. Also a series of illustrated talks and fringe events. For details contact the Festival Director at the address above.

Recordings of music heard at the concerts will be available under the B'nai B'rith Music Festival label. Catalogues on request from Jewish Music (Distribution) – see page 152.

Cameo Players
c/o Michael Sobell House, Limes Avenue, NW11   458 7411

An Anglo-Jewish theatre group performing light plays and comedies to raise money for charitable organizations. Formed in 1945, they put on plays in theatres and well-equipped synagogue halls. Performances are advertized in the *Jewish Chronicle*. They also have a playreading group for members.

Further details about membership or forthcoming events can be obtained from the address above.

Israel Folk Dance Association
134 Alderney Street, SW1   445 6765

A registered educational charity formed in 1979 to promote Israeli and Jewish dance in the UK. Whether you're a beginner or an expert, there should be a dance class in your part of London.

Membership of IFDA entitles you to discounts on admission to various classes, fees for seminars and the annual summer camp. You'll also receive the *Israel Folk Dance Quarterly*. IFDA do courses on cassette and video, too.

Jewish Music (Distribution)
P.O. Box 232, Harrow, Middx   907 1905

A specialist company which distributes music of Jewish interest by top artists by mail order, through record shops and in Jewish shops.

Its catalogue contains cassettes from the B'nai B'rith Music Festival (see previous page), plus sections for classical music which include Shostakovitch's Yiddish Song Cycle, Jewish Settings by Ravel, Bloch's Sacred Service, Wilfred Josephs' Kaddish Requiem and baroque Jewish music; also Jewish works by Leonard Bernstein and several Israeli composers.

In the cantorial and liturgical section you'll find records by the Zemel Choir (see opposite) and several eminent British cantors such as Louis Berkman, a baritone singing works by Sulzer and Lewandowski, and even a record by a woman cantor from America named Dora Krakower.

There are recordings of Hebrew and Yiddish songs, music from the 12th–18th centuries and various ethnic groups singing, for example, Sephardi songs from the Balkans.

There are also beautifully packaged cassettes and records for children, accompanied by booklets of well-known Israeli songs celebrating Yom Hatzmaut (Israel's Independence Day), all the Jewish festivals, Jerusalem, Shabbat, etc.

All music is available by mail order from the above address or from Manor House Books, 80 East End Road, N3; Blue and White Shop, 6 Beehive Lane, Ilford, Essex; HMV, Oxford Street, W1; branches of Our Price Records; Selfridges, Oxford Street, W1.

London Jewish Male Choir

Hon Secretary B. A. Hornick, 16 Charlton Road, Kenton, Middx   204 6069 (evenings)

This choir was formed in 1926 and celebrated its Diamond Jubilee in April 1986 with a major concert at the Queen Elizabeth Hall on the South Bank.

Over the past 60 years it has had four conductors, the present one being Julian Shindler, who is studying for the Rabbinate. Members of the choir are amateurs and come from all walks of life.

The choir has performed Jewish liturgical and secular music in all the major concert halls in Great Britain, as well as having toured Israel, the USA, West Germany and Ireland, often with distinguished guest singers, such as the late Jan Peerce, and well-known chazans (cantors). It has also performed on radio and television.

London Jewish Theatre Company

c/o E. Mendleson, 7 Newton Court, 35 Fairfax Road, NW6 328 9337

Founded in January 1983, this group aims to put on plays on Jewish themes to as wide an audience as possible. Professional casts are a mixture of Jewish and non-Jewish actors, but plays are about Jewish culture such as Arnold Wesker's *Chicken Soup with Barley*, or simply a Purim story.

Oranim

c/o IFDA, 134 Alderney Street, SW1   445 6765

This is a dance troupe whose colourful dance and music reflects the different influences which make up the Israeli cultural mosaic – Chasidic, Yemenite, Arabic and Armenian. The troupe was formed in 1979 and since then has appeared at the Queen Elizabeth Hall, the Labour Party Conference(!), and various multi-cultural and Jewish events. Members are dance enthusiasts who study or work in the London area.

Yiddish Theatre Group

This company performs plays in Yiddish for charity organizations. They have been in existence for 25 years and their 'season' runs from October to Pesach (Passover). Events are advertised in the *Jewish Chronicle*.

Zemel Choir

c/o Hendon Synagogue, Raleigh Close, NW4   202 6924

This choir was founded in 1955 by Dudley Cohen and specializes in Israeli folk and Jewish liturgical music. It has a professional conductor and accompanist.

The choir appears regularly at the Queen Elizabeth Hall and has taken part in many major festivals, including the International Eisteddfod in Wales and the Zimriya in Israel. It has given concerts at Westminster Abbey, appeared on television, and performed in America, Canada, Holland and Switzerland.

London Landmarks

NORTH LONDON/NORTH-WEST LONDON

Barnet Town Hall, NW4

In The Burroughs, Hendon. Has a statue outside called 'Family of Man' by Israeli sculptor Itzhak Ofer. It was a gift to the borough from the Rayne Foundation, to commemorate the twinning of the London Borough of Barnet with the Municipality of Ramat Gan in Israel. It was unveiled by the Prime Minister, the Rt Hon Mrs Margaret Thatcher, in 1981 (5741). The foundry was I. Zakensberg of Ramat Gan.

Golders Green, NW11

One of Jewish London's most popular shopping areas, full of fashion and food, and especially busy on Sundays. Each Chanucah, the Chasidic residents of the area erect a giant menorah outside Golders Green Station, its candles lit by well-known people who have to be hoisted up to the right level by crane!

Highgate Cemetery, N6

Particularly famous for its bust of Karl Marx (1818–83) who is buried here. Though born of Jewish parents, Marx was baptized when he was six.

The Jews' Free School, NW1

Now situated in Camden Town, was originally founded in 1817 by the Great Synagogue.

Stamford Hill, N16

Contains a large number of Chasidic *shtiblech* and yeshivot. Here you'll see Chasidic families – men in long black coats and wide hats, with curling sidelocks, and women wearing *sheitels* (wigs). There are also many North African, Indian and Persian Jews in this area.

EAST LONDON/EAST END

There are few reminders of the Jewish East End today. Many streets, like Black Lion Yard – East End's Hatton Garden – have been knocked down to make way for new factories or housing estates.

The Spitalfields Great Synagogue, on the corner of Fournier Street and Brick Lane, is now a mosque bearing not a single trace of its former existence. There is no Number 3, Princelet Street, where the first Yiddish theatre used to stand and where, on 18 January 1887, 17 people were crushed to death after a false cry of fire. And Adler House, Adler Street, once home of the Chief Rabbi, is now a leatherware company.

The Jewish clothing workshops are now occupied by immigrants from Pakistan and Bangladesh, only the occasional mezuza on the doorpost giving a clue to previous owners.

Even Petticoat Lane stalls no longer serve local customers – their Jewish clients travel down to the East End from comfortable homes in the suburbs, as do the stallholders themselves.

The air is filled with the spicy aroma of curry, and the only music you can hear is Indian. So for those who want a glimpse of the old East End, it's best to take a guided walking tour (companies offering such a service are listed on pages 160–2).

The following are landmarks you would see on your own . . .

A drinking fountain opposite the London Hospital, E1

Erected by the Jews of East London in 1911 as a memorial to King Edward VII. It's just outside the entrance to Whitechapel Underground Station, but on weekdays may well be obscured by market stalls.

An old synagogue in Princelet Street, E1

Built in 1862 over the garden of a former Huguenot silk-weaver's home at number 19. The house itself became a school. Jews who belonged to the Princelet Street Synagogue were mainly poor and worked in the garment trade, and the synagogue itself is tiny and simple. It was abandoned in 1963 and has been partially restored by The Heritage Centre, who have created a museum and cultural centre dedicated to the immigrants of the area – the Huguenots, Jews and Bengalis.

The soup kitchen for the Jewish poor

Established in 1902 at 17–19 Brune Street, E1, it still opens on Tuesday mornings to hand out food for the Jewish poor and is maintained by charitable aid.

A commemorative plaque on the Cunard Building

Records the site of the first synagogue after the Resettlement, 1657–1701. The synagogue was a house rented by the Marranos, Sephardi Jews (see page 8), and was replaced by Bevis

Marks Synagogue. The Cunard Building is on the corner of Creechurch Lane and Bury Street, E1.

A commemorative plaque on International House

Records the site of the Great Synagogue, Duke's Place, E1, a constituent of the United Synagogue. It was destroyed in September 1941 by bombing. The plaque can be found in Duke's Place, near St James's Passage.

Ridley Road, E8

In Dalston, once a popular Jewish market and still has a small Jewish following.

A painting of Rudolf Rocker in the Whitechapel Library

This hangs above the staircase. Rocker, who lived from 1873–1958, was a libertarian, philosopher, trade union organizer and leader of the Jewish immigrant poor. He lived in Whitechapel, E1, from 1895–1914.

Bevis Marks Synagogue

Britain's oldest synagogue, established in 1701. It was apparently built by a Quaker, Joseph Avis, who returned all the profit he made because he would not make money from building a house of God.

Queen Anne is credited with donating an oak beam from a warship to be used as a girder in the roof.

Bevis Marks is unusual in having windows on all four sides, and the only colouring being the blue around the east windows. It has seven candelabra, which represent the seven days of the week, ten large candlesticks, and 12 pillars supporting the gallery, which represent the 12 sons of Jacob. Electric light has now been installed but when candles are used it takes an hour and a half to light them all.

The magnificent wooden Ark at the east end contains the scrolls of the five books of Moses, the Hebrew letters above it indicating the Ten Commandments.

A famous worshipper at Bevis Marks was Sir Moses Montefiore, described as 'the most famous Jew in the world'.

Born in 1784 he lived to be 101, having made a fortune as one of the 12 Jewish brokers allowed on the Royal Exchange and using much of that money to help Jews both in England and abroad.

He was chosen as a Sheriff of London in 1837 and knighted at the Guildhall.

Petticoat Lane, E1

London's most famous street market, concentrated around Middlesex Street and Wentworth Street. Petticoat Lane was once the centre of the 'slop trade', as the second-hand clothes trade was known. Today stalls sell everything from fruit and hardware to clothing and umbrellas. Sunday morning is the time to visit.

THE CITY

The City was once home to a large Jewish population but there is little to record this now. The following are places or buildings of historic interest.

Old Jewry, EC2

The London ghetto before Edward I expelled the Jews in 1290. There used to be synagogues in this street, although today there are only financial institutions.

Jewry Street, EC3

This became the home of many Jews who escaped from rioting mobs at the time of Richard I's coronation.

The Old Bailey, EC4

Has a mural over Court 1 entitled 'Homage to Justice', including the figure of Dr Hermann Adler (1839–1911) who became Chief Rabbi in 1891 and was a leading spokesman for British Jewry.

The Rothschild Headquarters

In St Swithin's Lane, EC4; has a number of Rothschild portraits as well as a large tapestry of Moses striking the rock.

Incidentally, London's tallest building – the National Westminster Bank's NatWest Tower in Old Broad Street, EC2 – was designed by controversial Jewish architect, Richard Seifert.

SOUTH LONDON

Bowater House, Knightsbridge, SW1

Underneath it, at the entrance to Hyde Park, is a hunting scene in bronze by sculptor Sir Jacob Epstein (1880–1959). He had a studio nearby, at 18 Hyde Park Gate, only a few doors away from the town house of Sir Winston Churchill.

The Cenotaph

In Whitehall, SW1, is the site of a service on Remembrance Sunday (the second Sunday in November) to honour those who died for Britain in the two world wars. The march by ex-servicemen to the Cenotaph includes members of AJEX, Jewish Ex-servicemen.

Westminster Abbey, SW1

Has a section called Poets Corner. One poet commemorated is Isaac Rosenberg (1890–1918), famous for his paintings and poems of the First World War.

WEST LONDON/WEST END

Margaret Street, W1

In the West End, behind Oxford Street, is the heart of the clothing industry which was originally occupied mainly by Jewish manufacturers. Today it is a mixture of all races.

Soho, W1

Once the home of a large Jewish population, mainly engaged in tailoring and shopkeeping. Today all that remains are a few Jewish shops and salt beef bars.

Hyde Park, W1

In the part of Hyde Park known as The Dell is the Holocaust memorial garden dedicated to the Six Million. This was given to the Board of Deputies by the British Government in June 1983. The centre-piece is designed by Jewish architect Richard Seifert.

At Speakers' Corner you'll often hear people on soap-boxes defending or condemning Israel. And near Queen Anne's Alcove is a bird sanctuary set up as a memorial to the naturalist W. H. Hudson, which incorporates Jacob Epstein's controversial 'Rima' statue, which was twice tarred and feathered after its erection in 1925.

Sightseeing Tours

One of the best ways to see the East End and learn about its Jewish history is to join an organized sightseeing tour. Expert guides will be able to help you capture the atmosphere of the area as it once was, with anecdotes about life in those days, organizations and buildings that once existed in the East End.

The following organizations offer walking tours or other sightseeing services.

British Tours

6 South Molton Street, W1   629 5267

This company offers a variety of individual tours with driver/guide, and could arrange specific tours of Jewish London.

Bill Fishman

The most famous Jewish East End tour guide is social historian Bill Fishman, who has written books about the area. He takes groups of visitors and academics on walking tours of the East End, usually on weekdays, and can be contacted on 907 5166.

London Suburban Tours

158 Hamilton Avenue, Barkingside, Ilford, Essex   554 2904

This company takes walking tours round the East End on most Sundays of the year. Apart from visiting historic buildings, guides will give details of some of the famous people who lived in the East End of London, such as Jack Adelaide, Abie Saplestein, etc, and of the Yiddish theatres, the Yiddish Post Office, the area of the ghetto and the different immigrant groups. There is no need to book – just turn up (at Aldgate Underground Station, opposite the bus station, at 11 am). Can also arrange your own personal guide for a tour. Special rates for groups, students, unemployed and senior citizens. Walks last 2–2½ hours, and guides are all qualified 'blue badges' and historians.

Museum of the Jewish East End

The Manor House Centre for Judaism, 80 East End Road, N3 346 2288

Organizes sightseeing tours on foot for groups, which usually take place on Sunday mornings.

Prestige Tours

3 Elystan Street, SW3   584 3118 (24 hours)

A tour company offering personal sightseeing services by taxi, car or on foot. All members are qualified London Tourist Board guides and experienced London taxi drivers. The company particularly caters for groups with speciality interests, and will organize a tour of the Jewish East End, taking in Bevis Marks (London's oldest synagogue), the Sephardic part of London, the Jewish Museum, even North-West London if time permits. They will take you for a Jewish lunch at Bloom's, too!

If you prefer to 'go it alone', you might find a map of the Jewish East End handy. The Springboard Trust, 32 Foscote Road, NW4 (202 7147) produce one which can be obtained from them or from Tower Hamlets Library, 277 Bancroft Road, E1 (980 4366).

Who Lived Where?

Jewish writers, painters and politicians are among the many famous historical figures whose London homes are commemorated by Blue Plaques.

The idea of erecting plaques to mark the residences of famous people was first suggested by an anonymous correspondent in the *Journal of the Royal Society of Arts* back in 1864.

As a result, the Society set up a Committee on Memorial Tablets. In 1901 the London County Council launched its own commemorative plaques scheme and took over the work. Its work was continued by the Greater London Council (GLC), and plaques now appear as far afield as Bexley, Croydon and Redbridge.

Plaques commemorating Jewish figures can be found at the following addresses.

NORTH LONDON

20 Maresfield Gardens, NW3
Sigmund Freud (1856–1939), founder of psychoanalysis, lived here 1938–39. The plaque was erected in 1956.

EAST LONDON

32 Elder Street, E1
Mark Gertler (1891–1939), painter, lived here. The plaque was erected in 1975.

288 Old Ford Road, E2

Israel Zangwill (1864–1926), writer and philanthropist active in the Jewish Historical Society, lived here. The plaque was erected in 1965.

SOUTH LONDON

Hogarth House, Paradise Road, Richmond

Leonard Woolf (1880–1969), author and socialist, and husband of Virginia, lived here between 1912–24. He founded the Hogarth Press in 1917.

WEST LONDON

19 Curzon Street, W1

Benjamin Disraeli, Earl of Beaconsfield, died here in 1881. The plaque was erected in 1908.

32 Curzon Street, W1

Rufus Isaacs, 1st Marquess of Reading (1860–1935), lawyer and statesman, lived and died here. The plaque was erected in 1971.

28 Dean Street, W1

Karl Marx (1818–1883), German social philosopher, lived here 1851–56. The plaque was erected in 1967.

22 Theobalds Road, WC1

Benjamin Disraeli, Earl of Beaconsfield, was born here. The plaque was erected in 1948.

32 Craven Street, WC2

Heinrich Heine (1799–1856), German poet and essayist, lived here in 1827. His works include *Hebraische Melodien* and the unfinished novel *Der Rabbi von Bacherach*. The plaque was erected in 1912.

27 Stamford Brook Road, W6

Lucien Pissarro (1863–1944), painter, printer and wood engraver, lived here. The plaque was erected in 1976.

Historic Cemeteries

A full list of cemeteries and their addresses appears on pages 171–3.

Alderney Road

This site was bought by Benjamin Levy in 1696 for the Ashkenazi community. The lease cost him £190.

Near the entrance is a memorial tombstone for the founders, lay leaders and rabbis of the Ashkenazi community in London, who include **Benjamin Levy** himself (who died in 1705); **Moses Hart** (1675–1756), his son-in-law, who with profits from the South Sea Bubble paid to rebuild the Great Synagogue in 1722 so that it became known as 'Moses Hart's Shul', and also bequeathed money to the London Hospital in Whitechapel; **Aaron Hart** (1670–1756), the first Chief Rabbi of the Ashkenazi community in Britain, from 1709–56; **David Tevele Schiff**, Chief Rabbi from 1765 until his death in 1792, and generally recognized as the Chief Ashkenazi Rabbi in England; and **Samuel Falk** (*c.* 1708–82), a Cabbalist known as the Baal Shem of London and who had a reputation for being a 'miracle worker'.

Other figures buried in this cemetery include **Philas Franks** (1722–65), a great beauty who was painted by both Gainsborough and Reynolds, and **David Levy** (1740–99) who published a number of Jewish books including a Hebrew grammar.

Brady Street

This cemetery was leased to the New Synagogue in 1761 for an annual rent of 12 guineas (£12.60). It has been closed to burials since 1858.

In Jewish law, coffins must be separated by a distance of six hands' breadth, and only one body buried in each grave at least six feet from the surface. Brady Street soon became full, and as a result new earth was put over the area occupied by Jews who had belonged to no particular congregation, and more people buried above them. This area was called Strangers' Ground and still looks hilly today, with headstones placed back to back.

Famous historical figures buried in Brady Street cemetery include **Abraham Goldsmid** (1756–1810), who with his brother Benjamin was one of the leading members of the London money-market – they both committed suicide; **Rabbi Solomon Herschell** (1762–1842), who was born in London and returned there in 1802 as rabbi of the Great Synagogue. His authority as Chief Rabbi was formally recognized by the Ashkenazi communities throughout Britain; **Hyman Hurwitz** (1770–1844), professor of Hebrew at London University and a friend of poet and philosopher Samuel Taylor Coleridge; **Moses Jacob**, a founder of the New Synagogue; **Miriam Levey** (1801–56), who opened the first soup kitchen for the poor in Whitechapel; and **Nathan Mayer Rothschild** (1777–1836), founder of the English house of Rothschild. Rothschild settled in Manchester in 1798 before moving to London in 1805. Partly due to his family connections abroad, he helped fund the Government during the Napoleonic Wars.

East Ham

The first person to be buried here, in 1919, was a sailor called Able Seaman Jacob Emanuel. Also buried in this cemetery are **Isidore Berliner** (1869–1925), founder and president of the London Jewish Hospital; **Ted 'Kid' Lewis** (1893–1970), real name Gershon Mendeloff, who became world champion welter weight boxer in 1915; and Labour MP for Lambeth **Marcus Lipton** (1900–78).

Hackney

Opened in 1788, this originally belonged to the Hambro' Synagogue and was closed to burials in 1886. Graves include those of **Isaac Valentine** (1822–98), founder of the Jewish Orphan Asylum, and **Morris van Praagh** (1809–71), a president of the Hambro' Synagogue.

Hoop Lane

The east side of this cemetery is the Sephardi side, the west belongs to the West London Synagogue. The cemetery was founded in 1895.

Sephardi graves include those of **Arthur Blok** (1882–1974), principal examiner of HM Patents Office and the first director of the Israel Institute of Technology; English author and scholar **Philip Guedalla** (1889–1944), best known for his series of witty historical and biographical works; and **Stanley Setty** (1902–49), a car dealer murdered by Donald Hume (his dismembered torso was discovered wrapped in a carpet in the Essex marshes after it had been thrown from an aeroplane).

Graves on the west side include **Emanuel Belilios** (1837–1905), a member of Hong Kong's Legislative Council from 1882–1900; **Lord Leslie Hore-Belisha** (1893–1957), Liberal MP for Devonport and later Minister of Transport; **Sir Frederic Cowen** (1852–1935), musician and composer who wrote songs, instrumental music, operas and oratorios and became conductor of the London Philharmonic Society in 1887–92 and 1900–07; **Sir Basil Henriques** (1890–1961), a social worker who founded the Bernhard Baron St George's Jewish Settlement, and was an authority on juvenile deliquency; **Gerald Rufus Isaacs** (1889–1960), 2nd Marquess of Reading, a barrister who became Minister of State for foreign affairs, 1953–57, and was particularly involved during the Suez Crisis of 1956; **Sir Albert Levy** (1864–1937), benefactor of the Royal Free Hospital in Hampstead, NW3, and the Eastman Dental Hospital in Gray's Inn Road, WC1; **Baron Sterling Nahum** (1906–56), well known for his photographs of the Royal Family and official photographer at the Queen's Coronation in 1953; Jamaica-born **Sir John Simon** (1818–97), who became an English barrister and was made Serjeant-at-Law in 1868, and as Liberal MP between 1872 and 1892 championed Jewish causes outspokenly in the House of Commons, especially at the time of the Russian persecutions; and **Sir Frederick Stern** (1884–1967), a banker and horticulturalist who became chairman of the John Innes Horticultural Institute in 1947.

Kingsbury Road

This disused cemetery, founded in 1840, was once the burial

ground of many prominent Jewish families. Graves include those of **Sir Isaac Goldsmid** (1778–1859), created Baron de Palmeira in Portugal in 1846, the first Jew to be made a baronet, in 1841, and a founder of University College London; **Joseph Levy** (1811–88), a printer who founded the *Daily Telegraph*; **David Woolf Marks** (1811–1909), religious reformer and minister of the London Reform Synagogue for nearly 76 years; and **David Mocatta** (1803–82), a founder of the West London Synagogue.

Of the 42 burials recorded in the years up to 1853, it is interesting to note that seven were stillbirths and the average age of the remainder was just 33.

Liberal Jewish Cemetery

This cemetery is owned by the Liberal Jewish Synagogue in St John's Wood and has the graves of a number of well-known historical figures, including **Israel Abrahams** (1858–1925) who, with Claude Montefiore, founded and edited the *Jewish Quarterly Review* 1888–1908. An active supporter of Liberal Judaism in England, Abrahams served on the faculty of Jews' College from 1891–1902 before becoming reader in rabbinics at the University of Cambridge.

The cemetery also houses the cremated remains of author **Israel Zangwill** (1864–1926), famous for his stories about life in the East End. He was an active Zionist and founded the Jewish Territorial Organization. He also supported the suffragette and pacifist movements and was a member of the Jewish Historical Society.

Nuevo Synagogue

This is situated to the east of the old Sephardi cemetery, and was called The Cherry Tree because of the orchard that grew there. It was purchased in 1725, the orchard cut down to make way for a mortuary building (which was demolished in 1922), and the ground walled ready for burials.

For over 100 years almost all Sephardi burials took place in this cemetery, including those of prominent members of the community such as **Diego Pereira** (circa 1690–1759), adviser to Maria Theresa of Austria, who created him Baron Aguiler;

Sampson Gideon (1699–1762), a financier who during the Anglo-French wars in the mid-18th century was the principal agent for the raising of government loans and whose advice helped preserve England's financial stability during the Jacobite Rebellion in 1745 and the Seven Years' War; **Solomon da Costa Atias** (1690–1769), whose Hebrew library is now in the British Museum; **David 'Don' Pacifico** (1784–1854), the Gibraltar-born merchant whose claims for compensation when his property in Athens was pillaged by antisemitic rioters in 1847 resulted in Lord Palmerston's famous *Civis Romanus Sum* speech in the House of Commons ('A British subject shall feel that the strong arm of England will protect him'); and **Daniel Mendoza** (1764–1836), boxing champion of England from 1792–95.

An adjacent plot was bought in 1849 which served for another 50 years until the Golders Green Cemetery was acquired.

Much of the cemetery was destroyed by bombing during the Second World War and in 1974 the original Cherry Tree plot was sold to Queen Mary College for redevelopment, all the remains being transferred to Brentwood. Today only around 2,000 19th- and 20-century graves remain.

Queen's Elm Parade

This ground was bought by the Westminster Synagogue in 1815 to create the first Jewish burial ground west of the City. It was closed to burials in 1884.

Graves include those of **Solomon Hart** (1806–81), the son of a Plymouth silversmith, who became professor of painting at the Royal Academy 1854–63 – the first Jewish Royal Academian – and was noted for his canvases depicting dramatic historical scenes such as the 1655 Whitehall Conference to discuss the readmission of the Jews; **Zadok Jessel** (1792–1864), the father of **Sir George Jessel**, the first professing English Jew to hold political office; and **Jacob Waley** (1818–73), professor of political economy at University College London, and the first president of the Anglo-Jewish Association, 1871–73.

Rowan Road

Founded in 1915, this is the cemetery of the West End Chesed V'Emeth Burial Society. Most of those buried here came from

Eastern Europe and settled in the Soho area of London where they worked as tailors, cabinet makers and shopkeepers. The cemetery has been superseded by a new one at Cheshunt.

Velho Cemetery

This is the old Sephardi cemetery, founded in 1657 and the oldest Jewish burial ground in Britain. The Mile End Road site was acquired after the Sephardi community had successfully petitioned Oliver Cromwell for permission to establish a synagogue and cemetery.

The first person to be buried in this cemetery was **Mrs Isaac de Brito** in 1657. The Churchwardens of St Katharine Cree tolled their bell for this funeral and lent a pall for a fee of 2/4d (approximately 12p today). A stone slab in the present wall records the event.

Many Great Plague victims were buried here in the 1660s, as were an incredible number of children – there are over 600 entries in the registers prefixed *el angelito*, which denotes the burial of a child.

Graves include those of **Antonio Carvajal** (*c*. 1590–1659), who founded the modern English Jewish community – he furnished the Parliamentary forces with supplies during the Civil War and gave valuable political intelligence to Oliver Cromwell – and this cemetery ground was leased to him; **Simon de Caceres** (died in 1704), leader of the London Marrano community and one of the signatories of the petition of 1656–57 requesting toleration of the practice of Judaism in England; **Fernando Mendes** (who died in 1724), a Marrano physician who accompanied Catharine of Braganza to England when she came to marry Charles II, and who attended the king in his last illness; and **David Nieto** (1654–1728) who became Haham of the Sephardi community in London in 1702.

Western Synagogue Cemetery

Founded in 1884, this cemetery has the grave of **Samuel Montagu, Lord Swaythling** (1832–1911). He founded Samuel Montague & Co, one of the most important private banks in London, was a Liberal MP for many years, and was created Lord Swaythling in 1907. He also founded the Federation of Synagogues in London in 1887.

West Ham

In 1857 the New Synagogue and the Great Synagogue joined together to buy a five-acre site adjoining the West Ham municipal cemetery.

At the end of the central avenue stands an impressive mausoleum built in 1866 for **Evelina de Rothschild**, who died in childbirth at the age of 27. It was designed by Sir Matthew Digby Wyatt, and has the name Eva and the intertwined initials ER woven into its design. Her husband **Ferdinand** (1839–98), an art collector, is buried beside her. Ferdinand de Rothschild endowed the Evelina Children's Hospital, part of Guy's Hospital in Southwark, in memory of his wife.

Other graves include those of **Sir Benjamin Phillips** (1810–89), who was the first Jew to be elected as a common councilman in London and later became Lord Mayor in 1865; **David Salomons** (1797–1873), a founder of the London and Westminster Bank, who fought for Jews to be allowed to hold public office. Salomons became London's first Jewish sheriff in 1835, alderman in 1844, and the first Jewish Lord Mayor of London in 1855–56. A Liberal MP for Greenwich 1859–73, he was elected to the House of Commons in 1851 but was ejected from his seat since he refused to take the Christological oath.

Willesden

Founded in 1873, and with around 60,000 monuments, this is the burial place of some of the most important Jewish families in England. It was designed by Nathan Joseph, a Jewish architect.

People buried here include **Nathan Marcus Adler** (1803–90), grandson of David Tevele Schiff (see Alderney Road cemetery), and Chief Rabbi of England from 1845–90; **Isaacs Barnato** (1852–97), a conjurer who became a diamond merchant and with Cecil Rhodes founded the De Beers Consolidated Diamond Mines. He later turned to gold-mining and committed suicide by jumping overboard from a ship in mid-Atlantic; **Marcus Bearsted**, 1st Viscount (1853–1927), an English industrialist who created and subsequently developed the Shell Oil Company, was appointed Lord Mayor of London in 1902–03 and was raised to the peerage in 1920; **Sir Israel Brodie** (1895–1979), Chief Rabbi of the United Hebrew Congregations of the British Commonwealth from 1948–65;

businessman and financier **Sir Charles Clore** (1904–79) – a pavilion in London Zoo bears his name; **Sir Anthony de Rothschild** (1810–76), the first president of the United Synagogue; **Mayer de Rothschild** (1818–74), an MP and race-horse owner who won the Derby in 1871; **Joseph, Lord Duveen of Millbank** (1869–1939), a benefactor of the British Museum, the Tate Gallery and the National Portrait Gallery; and **Sir Israel Gollancz** (1864–1930), professor of English at King's College, London, 1905–30, one of the foremost Shakespearian experts of his day, and secretary of the British Academy from its foundation in 1902.

Cemeteries Directory

UNITED SYNAGOGUE

Alderney Road, E1: Opened for the Great Synagogue in 1696 (now disused).

Brady Street, E1: Opened for the New Synagogue in 1761 and subsequently used also by the Great Synagogue (now disused).

Bushey: Little Bushey Lane, Bushey, Herts. Opened in 1947.

East Ham: Marlow Road, E6. Opened in 1919.

Hackney: Lauriston Road, E9. Opened for Hambro' Synagogue in 1788 (now disused).

Plashet: High Street North, E12. Opened in 1896.

Waltham Abbey: Skillet Hill, Waltham Abbey, Essex. Opened in 1960.

West Ham: Buckingham Road, Forest Lane, E15. Opened in 1857.

Willesden: Beaconsfield Road, NW10. Opened in 1873.

FEDERATION

Montague Road: Angel Road, Lower Edmonton, N18

Upminster Road North: Rainham, Essex

UNION OF ORTHODOX HEBREW CONGREGATIONS

Enfield: Carterhatch Lane, Enfield, Middx.

Silver Street: Cheshunt, Herts.

SEPHARDI

Dytchleys: Coxtie Green, Brentwood, Essex. Disused.

Edgwarebury Lane: Edgware, Middx. Jointly shared by the Congregation, West London Synagogue and the Union of Liberal and Progressive Synagogues. Has been in use since 1976.

Hoop Lane, NW11: Jointly shared by the Congregation and the West London Synagogue.

Nuevo Cemetery: 329 Mile End Road, E1. Opened in 1725 (now disused).

Velho Cemetery: 253 Mile End Road, E1. Opened in 1657, the oldest Jewish burial ground in the United Kingdom (now disused).

REFORM

Edgwarebury Lane: See above.

Hoop Lane, NW11: See above.

Kingsbury Road: Balls Pond Road, N1.

LIBERAL

Edgwarebury Lane: See above.

Liberal Jewish Cemetery: Pound Lane, NW10. Owned by the Liberal Jewish Synagogue, NW8.

OTHER CEMETERIES

Bullscross Ride: Cheshunt, Herts. Cemetery of Western Synagogue and West End Great Synagogue.

Queen's Elm Parade: Fulham Road, SW3. Cemetery of Western Synagogue (now disused).

Rowan Road: Greyhound Lane, SW16. Cemetery of West End Synagogue.

Western Synagogue Cemetery: Montagu Road, N18.

Accommodation

For general advice on finding an hotel in London, see page 179. The kashrut authorities (see page 25) may be able to give you names of other kosher hotels and guesthouses in London but here are two of the most popular.

Croft Court Hotel
Ravenscroft Avenue, NW11   458 3331, 455 9175, 455 7789
Licensed by London Beth Din
AA/RAC/English Tourist Board recommended

Moderately-priced kosher hotel situated in Golders Green, close to several synagogues, restaurants and Jewish stores. Run by the Shapira family since 1969, it offers bed and breakfast, with Shabbat dairy meals on request.

Single, double and family rooms available, with private bath and WC, telephone in all rooms, TV lounge, sun terrace and car parking space. Room available for small business conferences and social functions.

The hotel is five minutes' away from local Underground and bus stations, and within easy reach of Brent Cross shopping centre and Wembley Stadium and Complex.

Kadimah Hotel (bed and breakfast)
146 Clapton Common, E5   800 5960 and 800 1716
Licensed by Beth Din and Kashrus Commission

Situated in Stamford Hill. There are 20 rooms, each with a radio, and a TV lounge. Meals can be obtained on request. The owners add that guests are made welcome and to feel at home.

The Sternberg Centre for Judaism (see page 129) has a limited amount of residential accommodation for students, visitors from the provinces and guests from abroad.

Miscellaneous Organizations and Institutions

Anglo-Israel Archaeological Society
3 St John's Wood Road, NW8   286 1176

Affiliated to the Friends of the Hebrew University.

Anglo-Israel Association
9 Bentinck Street, W1   486 2300

Anglo-Israel Friendship Leagues and Societies
741 High Road, Finchley, N12   446 1477

Association of Jewish Ex-Servicemen and Women (AJEX)
Ajex House, 5a East Bank, Stamford Hill, N16   800 2844

Association of Jewish Women's Organizations in the United Kingdom
Woburn House, Upper Woburn Place, WC1   387 7688

Beth Din
Adler House, Tavistock Square, WC1   387 5772

This is the court of the Chief Rabbi.

Board of Deputies of British Jews
Woburn House, Upper Woburn Place, WC1   387 3952

Established in 1760, the Board of Deputies takes suitable action against every antisemitic occurrence in the country. It has a number of committees dealing with education and youth, foreign affairs, shechita, statistical and demographic research, etc.

British-Israel Chamber of Commerce
126–134 Baker Street, W1   486 2371

British Na'amat
21 Dean Street, W1   437 5154

Affiliated to the Zionist Federation and the World Movement of Na'amat, Pioneer Women.

Central Enquiry Desk
Woburn House, Upper Woburn Place, WC1   387 4044

Under the auspices of the Board of Deputies, gives information on Jewish organizations both in Britain and abroad, and has an index of 'all the organizations that matter'.

Children and Youth Aliyah Committee for Great Britain and Eire
College House, New College Parade, Finchley Road, NW3
586 9221

Child Resettlement Fund: Emunah
2b Golders Green Road, NW11   458 5411

Charity group that works for underprivileged children in Israel.

Committee for the Welfare of Iranian Jews in Britain
346 3121 (evenings)

Gives assistance on all aspects of living in Britain, offering information on status, accommodation, etc.

Council of Christians and Jews
48 Onslow Gardens, SW7   589 8854

Czechoslovak Jewish Aid Trust
31 Craven Street, WC2   731 5860

Helps Jews of Czechoslovak origin in need, with legal advice, etc.

El Al
193 Regent Street, W1   437 9255

Federation of Women Zionists in Great Britain and Ireland
105–107 Gloucester Place, W1   486 2691

This is the British branch of WIZO and a constituent of the Zionist Federation of Great Britain and Ireland.

Hashomer Hatzair
37 Broadhurst Gardens, NW6   328 2554

Herut Movement of Great Britain
71 Compayne Gardens, NW6   624 1035

Israel Government Tourist Office
18 Great Marlborough Street, W1   434 3651

Israel Students Association
Hillel House, 1–2 Endsleigh Street, WC1   388 7750

Jewish Agency for Israel
741 High Road, Finchley, N12   446 1477

Jewish Communal Marriage Bureau
529b Finchley Road, NW3   794 4779

Jewish Feminist Group
Box 39, Sisterwrite Bookshop, 190 Upper Street, N1

Jewish Gay Group
c/o North-Western Reform Synagogue, Alyth Gardens, NW11

Jewish Memorial Council
Woburn House, Upper Woburn Place, WC1   387 3081

Mapam – for a Progressive Israel
37 Broadhurst Gardens, NW6   328 2554

Mizrachi – Hapoel Hamizrachi Federation of Great Britain and Ireland
2b Golders Green Road, NW11   455 2243

Poale Zion – Labour Zionist Movement
62 Charles Lane, NW8   586 4433

Pro-Zion: Progressive Religious Zionists
The Manor House Centre for Judaism, 80 East End Road, N3
349 4731

Union of Jewish Students
Hillel House, 1–2 Endsleigh Street, WC1
387 4644 and 380 0111

World Zionist Organization
741 High Road, Finchley, N12   446 1477

Zionist Federation of Great Britain and Ireland
Balfour House, 741 High Street, Finchley, N12   446 1477

Tourist Information

Accommodation

Travel agents will be able to give you details of London hotels (kosher hotels are listed on page 174). You could also contact the English Tourist Board's Information Centre (see below).

Entertainment and Sightseeing

If you want to know what's on at the theatre or cinema, which events are happening while you're in London, etc, there are a number of publications which list them. These include *What's On and Where To Go in London*, *City Limits*, *Time Out*, and most newspapers – *The Times*, the *London Standard* (evening paper, Mon–Fri) and the *Sunday Times* are good. These are all available from newsagents and news-stands.

Details are also available from the English Tourist Board's Information Centre at Victoria Station, SW1 (730 3488); and the City of London Information Centre, St Paul's Churchyard, EC4 (606 3030), which publishes a monthly diary of City events.

Exhibitions and events are also advertized at Underground stations, on Capital Radio (MW 194 m, VHF/FM 95.8), and Radio London (MW 206 m, VHF/FM 94.9).

Half-price tickets for West End theatres are offered at the Ticket Booth in Leicester Square, W1, but you have to turn up in person and queue. Many theatres will take credit card bookings by phone.

Telephones

The minimum charge in public callboxes is 10p. When in London and dialling London numbers, omit the 01.

For the emergency services – police, fire brigade or ambulance – there is no charge. Dial 999.

British Telecom offers a number of information services, which are listed in the front of the A-D telephone directory. These include:

Leisureline
A daily selection of main events in and around London.
In English   246 8041
In French   246 8043
In German   246 8045

Children's London
Events and competitions   246 8007

FT City Line
Business news and FT Index   246 8026
International market reports   246 8086

Directory inquiries
For numbers in London dial 142.
For numbers outside London dial 192.

General inquiries
Dial the operator on 100.

You will also find useful local numbers, eg places of interest, theatres, airports, rail terminals, etc, listed in the front of the A-D directory.

Public Transport

The Underground

All tube stations display the times of their first and last trains (from the centre of London these are between 5.30 am and 12.15 am; 7.30 am–11.30 pm on Sundays). Fares depend on the number of zones you have to travel through. After 9.30 am you can buy a one-day travel pass which entitles you to travel 'free' on buses and tubes – from the suburbs this works out cheaper than buying a return ticket. Your local station will give full details of all the money-saving schemes available.

Buses

The first and last times of buses are indicated at bus stops (from the centre of London between 6 am–12 midnight; 7.30 am–11.30 pm on Sundays). Buses rarely arrive on time, so if in a hurry it's best to choose the Underground. Again, fares vary according to the number of zones travelled through.

On some buses you have to pay as you enter; on others a conductor comes round to collect the fares. Bus conductors may refuse to accept large notes so make sure you have plenty of coins.

At 'request' stops (with red signs), you have to hail buses by raising your arm. If on a bus, ring the bell, otherwise the bus won't stop.

Some buses run through the night – details from your local Underground station or the Travel Information Centre, St James's Park Station, SW1 (222 1234).

British Rail

Your travel agent should be able to give you details of train times and fares. There are British Rail Travel Centres at 4–12 Lower Regent Street, SW1; 14 Kingsgate Parade, Victoria Street, SW1; 87 King William Street, EC4; 407 Oxford Street, W1; 170b Strand, WC2; Heathrow Airport. Main stations also have their own information offices.

Taxis

Black cabs displaying the 'For Hire' sign can be hailed in the street by raising your arm. A meter will record the charges, which increase according to time and distance. On journeys which will take you outside the Metropolitan Police District, you will have to negotiate a price with the driver beforehand. Expect to pay extra for luggage, for journeys after 8 pm, and at weekends and bank holidays.

For your nearest rank look in the telephone directory under Taxi.

Mini-cabs

Details of local firms who will collect you and take you by car to your destination can be found in the Yellow Pages. There are no set charges for mini-cab journeys, nor do drivers display meters, so to avoid being over-charged you should always ask in advance how much the fare will be.

Car Hire

Car hire firms will be listed in the Yellow Pages telephone directory. Prices vary, so it's worth ringing a few to get the best deal. Avis, Budget, Hertz and other well-known companies have offices in London.

Remember that parking is illegal on double yellow lines at all times, and on single yellow lines at certain times of the day.

Shopping

Most shops open between 9 am or 9.30 am and 5 pm or 5.30 pm Monday to Saturday. Only small shops close for lunch. Large department stores and supermarkets often have late-night shopping on one day a week; Brent Cross Shopping Centre, NW4, a huge complex of major stores, is open until 8 pm Mon–Fri and until 6 pm Sat.

Many suburban grocers and delicatessens and selected shops are open on Sundays, particularly in Jewish areas. In addition, a large number of Asian-run grocery stores are open late most evenings.

Banks

Opening times are usually 9.30 am–3.30 pm Mon–Fri, although Israeli banks may be different (see page 80). Selected branches of the major banks are open on Saturday mornings. All banks close on national holidays.

There are also a large number of Bureaux de Change scattered throughout London, at or near main railway stations (eg Paddington, Euston, King's Cross), along major shopping routes (eg Oxford Street), and in some of the larger department stores.

Post Offices

These are usually open 9 am–5.30 pm Mon–Fri, and 9 am–12.30 pm Sat. Notable exceptions are the Post Office in King William Street, Trafalgar Square, WC2, which is open 8 am–8 pm Mon–Sat, and 10 am–5 pm Sun and bank holidays, and the Post Office in King Edward Street, EC1, which is open 8 am–7 pm Mon–Fri and 9 am–12.30 pm Sat. Some small local post offices close at lunchtime. Post offices are listed under 'P' in the L-R telephone directory.

Useful Addresses and Telephone Numbers

American Embassy
24 Grosvenor Square, W1   499 9000

Foreign Office
Clive House, Petty France, SW1   213 3000

Immigration Office
Lunar House, Wellesley Road, Croydon, Surrey   686 0688

Israeli Embassy
2 Palace Green, W8   937 8050

Lost Property Office
200 Baker Street, W1
Mon–Fri 9.30 am–5.30 pm (no telephone enquiries)

This deals with items left on London Transport. Other lost property should be reported to the local police station.

Emergencies

Fire, police and ambulance services
Dial 999.

Late-night medical help
Your local police station should be able to give details of chemists, doctors and dentists. Or phone Capital Radio's Help Line (388 7575).

Late night chemists include Bliss Chemist, 54 Willesden Lane, NW6; V. J. Hall, 85 Shaftesbury Avenue, W1; Warman-Freed, 45 Golders Green Road, NW11.

Personal problems
Contact The Samaritans, St Stephen's Church Crypt, EC4 (283 3400). Open 24 hours.

If you've been raped or sexually assaulted
Contact the Rape Crisis Centre (837 1600) for support and advice.

If you've been robbed
Report the incident to the police immediately. If a theft has occurred in your hotel, report it to the hotel management via the reception desk. If you passport has been stolen, contact your own embassy (details in the telephone directory).